THE BRITISH SEASON

THE BRITISH SEASON

MATTHEW COOK · PAUL DUNCAN

A CELEBRATION OF SUMMERTIME ENTERTAINMENTS

LITTLE, BROWN AND COMPANY

Boston · New York · Toronto · London

A LITTLE, BROWN BOOK
Published in association with Royal Mail

This edition first published in Great Britain in 1994
by Little, Brown and Company

A CIP catalogue record for this book
is available from the British Library

ISBN 0-316-90986-6

10 9 8 7 6 5 4 3 2 1

Designed by Andrew Barron and Collis Clements
Associates
Typeset in Berkeley O.S. by SX Composing Ltd,
Rayleigh, Essex
Printed and bound in Spain

Little, Brown and Company (UK) Ltd
Brettenham House, Lancaster Place
London WC2E 7EN

Royal Mail, British Philatelic Bureau
20 Brandon Street, Edinburgh EH3 5TT

CONTENTS

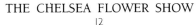

SUMMERTIME Cowes

SUMMERTIME Lord's

SUMMERTIME Braemar

INTRODUCTION

To MOST NATIVES of these islands the 'British Season' is traditionally synonymous with strange class rites enacted in fancy dress to the accompaniment of lashings of fizzy drinks and alfresco dining. It conjures up images of British Society milling about the cricket pitch or the paddock, perched by the picnic hamper or in the tea tent, fulfilling the habits of a lifetime in large hats or striped blazers, and not so much interested in the sport as getting on with the serious business of socializing. These rituals signal the upper classes at play; this is the essence of the British Season which, traditionally, belongs to the well-born. Yet an alternative exists — it always has. Side by side, inextricably enmeshed sometimes, the two provide the nation's annual entertainment, usually in the summer, and it is this entertainment that, in light-hearted fashion, is celebrated here.

Exclusivity has always been the hallmark of the British Season, for at its core is a series of events — Royal Ascot, the Cowes Regatta, the polo at Windsor, for example — at which the Royal Family goes public or, more accurately, mingles with that part of society with which it has some social and cultural affinity. In fact, this is one area of national life in which it is possible to observe the workings of the class system with great ease.

Once, in the Golden Age between the two world wars, there was a London Season and there was a Sporting Season. Both were adorned by Society. The stuff of an Evelyn Waugh novel, the principal hallmarks of the London Season were the court presentations of eligible young women jockeying for position in the marriage market, and the balls and parties which followed. There was even something called the 'Little Season', which marked the onset of winter. A Scottish Season heralded late summer's migration north of the border, its own peculiarities characterized by the frenzied slaying of beasts, fowl and fish and matched only by frenetic rounds of balls and dances. Then, as now, each Season's every event was accompanied by high ritual, tradition and etiquette, and dressing up to party and to play outdoors, whether in the saddle, shooting, or on the river bank, produced a great sense of theatre and of raffish excess and extravagance.

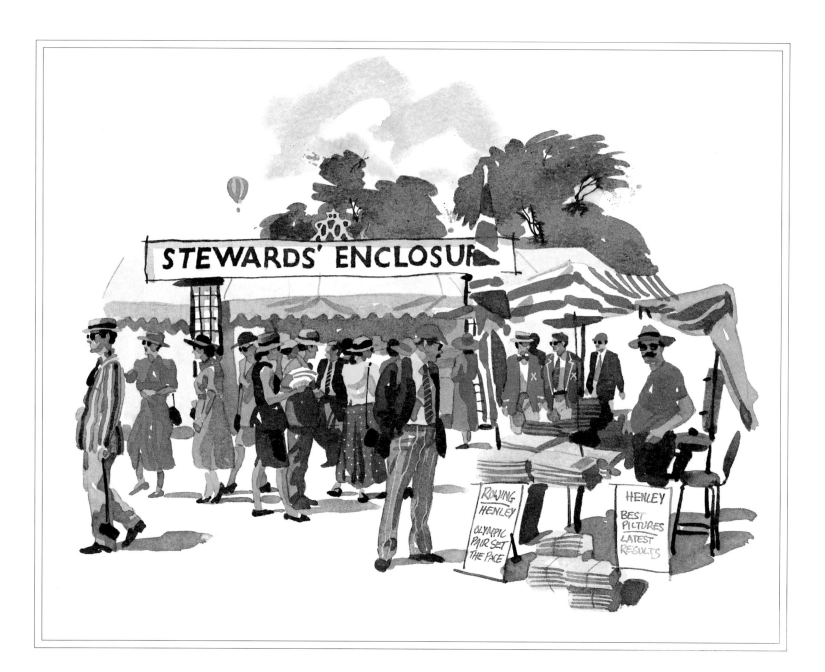

Yet nowadays there is an alternative to that quintessential Season. It might be called the 'People's Season'. While the Season proper appears to marginalize the bulk of the British public, there are plenty of other events which are marked out as its own particular turf — for example, the Illuminations at Blackpool, Alton Towers theme park, and country fairs up and down the land. And because the boundaries of that traditional Season have never been strictly demarcated — indeed, they are constantly in a state of flux — this book legitimately includes a range of events under the banner of what might be called 'The True British Season'.

This is the democratic version of what once belonged exclusively to Society, and may be read as the by-product of Prime Minister Major's classless society. And anyway, some events like the Derby, long bridging the gap between the two, have always belonged to everybody. Just as plenty of people from all walks of life visit stately homes open to the public not just to see how the other half live but to glimpse the especially English ensemble of the great house with its collections and grounds, so all classes of British society dissolve into one great blur at Epsom on Derby Day, their focus the enormously beguiling attractions of the richest race in the world. Whatever the event, its inclusion in the book derives from its importance to the Season's calendar and is as much of a fixture in it as strawberries are at Wimbledon and huge hats at Ascot's Ladies Day.

So, while we've donned our panamas and club ties for the Stewards' Enclosure at Henley and given our morning dress and top hat an airing at Ascot, we've also tramped through the mud with 199,998 others at the Royal Welsh Show, been rocketed into space on a monster roller coaster at Alton Towers and, with the day trippers, queued to admire Her Grace's four-poster at Chatsworth. In shorts and T-shirts with knotted hankies on our heads, we've watched Morris Dancers and sheepdog trials, and we've hung about on pavements watching street theatre at Edinburgh's Festival Fringe.

Instead of being purely London-based, which so many of the traditional Season's events are, this book actively seeks out those beyond the home counties in an effort to illustrate as fully as possible the British at play in this most precious of periods. And thus, because the British have an amazing propensity for reinventing themselves,

facilitating movement between the classes, and because the Season constantly shifts its boundaries, some events have been included for the first time.

Nowadays it is mostly sport (there are exceptions, as the book will point out — for example, the Chelsea Flower Show, the Royal Academy Summer Show and the Edinburgh Festival) that provides the occasion, though not necessarily the content, of the event. And however varied the make-up of the British Season, however subtle its nuances, the event is an excuse for the Great British alfresco meal, the picnic. Food and lashings of drink are paramount whether it is Ascot's lobster salad and champagne from the boot of the Rolls, sandwiches and a pint of ale on the green at the village cricket match, or fish and chips and a six-pack on the pier at Blackpool. Nothing tastes better than an outdoor meal consumed as a ritual. Rain or shine, play carries on regardless.

THE CHELSEA FLOWER SHOW

MAY

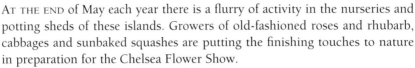

AT THE END of May each year there is a flurry of activity in the nurseries and potting sheds of these islands. Growers of old-fashioned roses and rhubarb, cabbages and sunbaked squashes are putting the finishing touches to nature in preparation for the Chelsea Flower Show.

The countdown begins a week from opening day. While, countrywide, sun lamps are gently nudging buds to open on cue, in the normally tranquil gardens of the Royal Hospital on Chelsea Embankment, a place more used to sheltering the scarlet-coated Chelsea Pensioners as they potter about their business, lorry-loads of workmen and women are transforming the lawns into fern-encrusted Victorian glades and woodland gardens, trimming hedges and laying cables, and delivering rocks and peat. One year they were spotted positioning a pump that artificially propelled waves in a seaside garden soon to be conjured out of twenty tons of imported sand dumped on a section just off the showground's Main Avenue. A Norfolk dune was the result.

The work is feverish. Tempers fray and nerves, already raw, are getting worse by the hour. Much is at stake: being selected for an award is the pinnacle of horticultural achievement and, unsurprisingly, this is one of the most keenly anticipated events of summertime, the nirvana of all plants and their keepers. Tennis players have Wimbledon and country house bores have Chatsworth, but this is show-time for the nation's gardeners and nothing, but nothing, can stop it from taking place.

The flower show has a wide variety of fans, ranging from monarch to vicarage wives in stout brogues and young married couples from the suburbs. Each comes for different reasons, but all are united by their shared interest in 'green' matters and a desire to learn more about them. And learn they will, since one of the roles of the show is to educate: there can be few places in London SW3 where a baobab tree from drought-stricken Zimbabwe can be seen. Rarer, the opportunity to follow up a sighting with a lesson in the relationship between global warming and the newly designed Drought Resistant Garden.

These good intentions are presided over by the Royal Horticultural Society, which has always delivered its message with missionary zeal. Founded in 1804, the Society's

first meeting, at Hatchard's in Piccadilly, vowed to make the knowledge of professional gardeners available to a wider public. The first exhibit shown was, endearingly, a potato. There is good reason, therefore, that one whole side of the much coveted Great Marquee exhibition space is devoted to deeply unfashionable educational exhibits dealing with, for example, Pershore College's Aspects of Earthworms, and the story of rhubarb — a stand diligently provides 150 varieties for inspection. But this is what draws the public and there is no greater magnet than the stands which break into virgin territory with new plants named, say, 'Gloria Hunniford' (a statuesque lupin) or 'Catherine Deneuve' (a fluffy astilbe which is more funeral corsage than first night). Even unpronounceables like the *yakushimanum* rhododendrons ('Hydon Pearl' and 'Desert Orchid' to you and me) seem to delight the enthusiasts.

But most of all, the Chelsea Flower Show makes a point of remembering the ordinary gardener. The three and a half acre marquee is divided into four segments representing dry and moist shade and dry and moist sun — in other words, all the extremes that the average gardener is ever likely to encounter. In addition, twenty-three specimen gardens make real virtually every suburban fantasy using interesting combinations as diverse as, say, French lavender and frilly red cabbages. There are endless nuances and possibilities and they can be discussed *in situ* with the brightest horticultural brains in the country. Favoured exhibits can be bought after the show — in the 1920s the Prince of Wales proudly carried off an entire rock garden to his home at Fort Belvedere. And, to keep the Chelsea show in line with other lesser shows, at Malvern or Holker, or at Hampton Court, a part of it is, reluctantly it seems, allotted to the manufacturers of conservatories who clamour petulantly for space around the Great Marquee. Mowing machines and other garden implements are relegated to stands around the periphery, along with the manure: 'Designer manure provides upward growth' is the modern cry, and the substitute for the guano fertilizer on sale earlier in the century.

The Chelsea Flower Show has had a rather chequered history. The first exhibition on this site opened in May 1912, the venue replacing the earlier Embankment Gardens site of the Inner Temple. There it had resided, squashed into a few acres, for twenty-five years until the fractious owners, infuriated by the cooking smells and the noise, decided that enough was enough and booted it out. Coincidentally, the site had already become too small for the RHS's needs anyway, particularly when, in 1910, it received over 1,400 applications for space in the Royal International Horticultural Exhibition. It subsequently moved to the Royal Hospital grounds, a site over three times as large as the previous one. There can be no better venue for a show which, held for four days in May when English gardens are springing to life, is a celebration of nature.

The Chelsea Flower Show has become a national institution and it has a designated slot in what's left of the official Season's calendar. But long gone are the days when exhibitors wore top hat and tails. The royal connections survive — Her Majesty the Queen makes an evening visit — but these links reverberate down the social scale with less vigour now than in the past. Then, Members' Day, if you belonged to the Royal Horticultural Society, was the time to come, and you were entitled to wander about quietly enjoying the displays or looking for ideas, your head gardener in attendance. Those who came were people who had gardens sprawled magnificently around some ancient seat — the kind which, by now, would have been opened to the public. These days anyone can be a member of the Society — you just enrol at the gate — and consequently Members' Day is as much of a scrum as any other. Her Majesty cannily avoids it, preferring to visit the show the day before it opens. The President's Tuesday afternoon tea party is the last vestige of former exclusivity, though now it tends to be the preserve of TV personalities with a penchant for gardening, with a sprinkling of grandees thrown in for old time's sake.

The success of the show derives in part from the RHS's lofty mission to inform — for which the public, judging by the clamour for tickets, is deeply appreciative. That this important event takes place on a tiny metropolitan site squashed between the river and a huge historic building and encircled by busy roads in the heart of a traffic-congested capital city, seems hardly to matter. That it is quirky and eccentric, that it still adheres to old traditions and keeps its royal appellation, are what's important. Without a balance of these, the Chelsea Flower Show would probably no longer exist.

INSIDER TIPS

❀ Leave dog and children at home. The Chelsea Flower Show doesn't welcome them.

❀ Arrival without a pre-booked ticket will result in disappointment: no tickets are sold at the gate.

❀ Be warned: there is nowhere to park your car in SW3, which is prime clampland, so it is advisable to leave it at home. It is best to go by public transport or by taxi.

❀ Late on the last day of the show you can buy the exhibits. Bring carrier bags or binliners — anything — so that you can carry away your booty.

❀ Bring a notebook and pen. Diagrams and Latin names will need recording.

THE ROYAL ACADEMY SUMMER EXHIBITION

MAY — JUNE

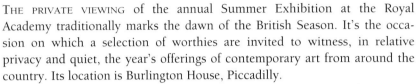

THE PRIVATE VIEWING of the annual Summer Exhibition at the Royal Academy traditionally marks the dawn of the British Season. It's the occasion on which a selection of worthies are invited to witness, in relative privacy and quiet, the year's offerings of contemporary art from around the country. Its location is Burlington House, Piccadilly.

Anyone, anywhere may submit an artwork — paintings in oil or watercolour, prints, miniatures, sculpture, architecture — for appraisal by a panel of the Academy's judges. If it passes their stringent examination, it will hang on the Academy's walls with nearly 2,000 others, there to be scrutinized, ridiculed or garlanded with honours. The lucky ones win a cash prize from one of nine awards. In 1993, out of over 13,000 entries, only 1,800 were chosen — though the word 'only' is used lightly. The hallowed galleries of the Royal Academy can barely cope even with that enormous amount.

The Summer Exhibition gives the Season's 'eventers' the chance to look in on what the contemporary art world is up to before the Society bandwagon heads for more appealing arenas: the cut-and-thrust of the racetrack, the champagne tent, or the killing fields of summer's annual massacre on the moors miles from London. It provides a metropolitan stage for gossip and idle chatter and is an opportunity, if these things mean much to you, to play the connoisseur for a day and deliver judgement for better or worse on the artistic merits of the nation's creative force.

But the most recent show — the 225th — wasn't quite the same as others in the past, at least as far as its 'seasonal' status is concerned. Perhaps this isn't surprising considering that over 35,000 people are entitled to call themselves 'Friends of the Royal Academy', all of whom are permitted to attend a private view — traditionally the preserve of Society. Without fail they all turn up to assert their right to know what is going on in the visual arts, and to do it in style with a sense of decorum at what has become the world's biggest 'festival' of contemporary art.

To cope, the Academy has invented three private view days to precede the exhibition's opening to the general public. Day One is, if anything, the grandest of the three

and to it you are invited if you've bought pictures from the exhibition in the past. This is the day on which you can see one or two remaining signs that the Summer Exhibition's status was once a fairly elevated one — part of the 'summer performance', said one critic sniffily. Remember those women you saw tottering down Piccadilly, their flowery hats perched on blue-rinsed hairdos, their strings of pearls jiggling as they went? They were the ones following the tradition of the summer show as our grandmothers will have known it, and had they been Lord Mayor they would have brought added dignity to the occasion by arriving in no less than a ceremonial coach. These are the exhibition's armed forces, the shires brigade, who religiously attend its opening year after year. It is they

who nod sagely at the hideous abstractions and the kitsch representations, mindful of the 'simple joy of the amateur', as Daniel Farson of the *Mail on Sunday* once put it. It is for these splendid ladies that the Summer Exhibition is as much a hallowed national ritual as a garden party at Buckingham Palace. But is this art that they come to see?

It is true that the quality of the exhibits varies tremendously. Much of it isn't even appealing — a 'pot pourri of mock Matisse and pseudo Picasso offering more than a touch of amusement for many', said one critic. Much of it is simply an enticement to slander and derision — two fashionably pejorative tones for contemporary criticism. This is 'the undergrowth of British painting', say some, 'a collection of Hyde Park railings rubbish', say others. But to have to ask that original question and, consequently, to have to answer it, is really to miss the point of the exhibition completely. Nothing here is meant to be taken seriously. In amongst the stars — in 1993 David Hockney exhibited six new paintings and there was work by Jasper

Johns and Roy Lichtenstein — there are other less known and unknown names and not all of their work is first rate. Nobody pretends that it is, because being an exhibitor is not necessarily a mark of artistic excellence, neither is exclusion from it a disgrace.

Quite simply, the exhibition is intended as a glorious celebration for people who know what they like. For some, like Irene of Bournemouth with her cat pictures and lack of formal training, to be chosen to hang in the exhibition is the pinnacle of achievement. This is a festival of the work of people like her, as well as of those more proficient at their art. And anyway, in the face of all that slander and derision, it is as well to remember that, in having a Summer Exhibition at all, the Royal Academy is fulfilling one of the key motives for which it was established in 1768: to allow ordinary mortals a chance to exhibit their work. The tradition is a long and hallowed one, though not as long or as old as the Royal Academy itself, of which the first President was the painter Sir Joshua Reynolds (1723–92). In his day it came into being because a group of worthies believed that the public ought to be taught the art of painting and given the chance to exhibit their own work. Keep well within your sights the one 'great duty of the Royal Academy', said one of its former Secretaries. This is 'to keep the main body of art alive, through regular intercourse with the perceptions and feelings of ordinary people — who must be familiar with the norms before they can appreciate the strange fruits of experiment'.

And so it is that for two and a half summer months, the seascapes and the *pointillist* pot plants, the wire-mesh sculptures and the grotesque plaster giants are allowed to adorn the halls of this hallowed establishment. The nudes conjured up during life-drawing classes at adult education centres stare triumphantly down at the viewers as if to say: 'We have a right to be here and don't you forget it.'

INSIDER TIPS

☛ The handling fee for entering works into the Summer Exhibition (maximum of three works each) is £10 for every work submitted.

☛ Become a Friend of the Royal Academy to attend a private view.

☛ There are reductions for parties of people wishing to see the exhibitions here, and there are others for families wishing to become Friends of the RA.

☛ Dress code: hats are not essential should you be invited to a private view.

☛ Most of the works on show are for sale, from as little as £200.

NO SINGLE EVENT on the Season's calendar is capable of depopulating London quite as much as the Derby Stakes at Epsom. Derby Day is hugely popular, a national event providing jubilation and disappointment in equal measure for countless numbers of people.

A horse is never a dead cert winner until it passes the finishing post — there are too many variables to ensnare it on the way. It might rain and the course might be soggy, which is good for some horses but hopeless for others. Equally, there might be a heat wave, in which case the course will be firm and resilient. Luck almost certainly plays a part: horses get into bad places approaching Tattenham Corner and sometimes never properly recover. Some don't like the severe pull of half a mile in the first part, while others can't do justice to the downhill work which follows. The Derby gives the horses a bit of everything and that is one of the reasons it has a reputation as the supreme test for the most brilliant three-year-olds of the season.

These and all the other variables make for a thrilling crowd-puller, exciting members of the Royal Family, London society, East Enders, gypsies and others alike, and the tension of Derby Day is felt as much by punters as by the horses. Unsurprisingly, the greatest ambition of every owner of racehorses, every trainer and every jockey, is to win the Derby, the prize money for which is enormous. On 4 May 1780, the inaugural Derby Stakes carried a purse of 1,075 guineas, the total entry fees subscribed by the owners of the thirty-six entrants. On 2 June 1993, the purse was £750,000 and the total value of the runners more than £25 million.

The 1993 Derby attracted more attention than usual for all kinds of reasons, some of them only indirectly related to horses. Two queens, a fifty-seven-year-old folk hero grandfather, and a starter with an infamous reputation were to blame, all of them smitten by the thrill of the greatest horse race in the world. Everybody knows that Her Majesty the Queen is horse mad. She breeds them, owns them, races them and rides them and in this, the fortieth anniversary of her coronation, a singular achievement and a landmark in modern history, she chose to spend the day watching them gallop around Tattenham

Corner at Epsom Racecourse on Derby Day. And why not? There are many people in the world who understand this most singular devotion of hers — more than 450 million are said to have joined her at their TV sets — but none better than the Queen Mother, who rallied after a debilitating illness to accompany her to the Royal Box, making this her first post-malady public engagement.

Royalty and the Derby have had an intermittently illustrious relationship. On Wednesday, 8 May 1788, the Prince of Wales's Sir Thomas won £971 15s. in the ninth Derby, marking the first success in that race of the royal colours. But not until 1900 did another Prince of Wales win, this time with a horse called Diamond Jubilee, a bad-tempered brute who ended his days in peaceful repose in Argentina. Since then, there have been no other royal winners, although Queen Elizabeth's horse Aureole brought her near to triumph in the Derby by coming second in 1953, the year of her coronation. That year was a memorable Derby; seldom can sympathies have been so divided between the two horses, Pinza and Aureole, that fought out the finish. Pinza was ridden by Gordon Richards, who had just been knighted and whose brilliant career lacked only a victory in the greatest race of the year; Aureole carried the colours of the newly crowned Queen. Pinza was the winner.

But royalty and their preferences for equine events were not the only reason for the lustre of the 1993 event. It was also the year in which folk hero Lester Piggott, by now a fifty-seven-year-old grandfather, chose to return, riding his thirty-fifth Derby in an effort to win the world's most celebrated horse race for the tenth time. His participation was the focus for much of the once-a-year money as he went to post on Fatherland, a horse trained by Piggott's old friend and six-times Derby winner, Vincent O'Brien. Piggott and O'Brien had already won four previous Derbys together and all the small punters and casual racegoers backed them again. One spokesman for a large firm of bookmakers predicted that a win for Piggott's mount 'would probably clean us out'. In the event, however, Fatherland finished ninth: 'He just didn't act on the track', said Piggott.

Win or no win, this world-famous jockey will always have highly favoured status in racing lore — unlike the hapless starter Captain Keith Brown, the man responsible for 'starting' the Grand National That Never Was (1993). The Derby has the horses starting

out of the stalls, which possibly renders the race less prone to mistakes than the National, where they line up behind a tape. It was starter Brown's last Derby before retirement but he too, in the event, walked into racing history without a blip, though not without much sarcastic speculation from the sporting press.

The Derby takes its name from the illustrious Stanleys, Earls of Derby, who have long featured prominently in the annals of both the history of England and the history of the Turf. Even in Lancashire, where they live, they occupy the position of local royalty; indeed the loyal Lancastrian's toast was 'God save the Earl of Derby and the King!' A great many of them seem to have achieved immortality for having backed winners, not all of them four-legged ones. The ancestors of the present Earl were skilled in backing the two-legged royal variety, therefore saving not only their proverbial 'bacon' but much else besides, including their heads. The Stanleys chose the right side of the field at Bosworth — the second Lord Stanley having been the stepfather of victorious Henry Tudor. He subsequently placed the crown on Tudor's head, transforming him into Henry VII. The third Earl, too, was a master of opportunity for, as one chronicler of the fortunes of the Stanleys once put it, 'Under Edward VI he acted as a Commissioner for the advancement of the Reformation; under Mary he delivered Protestants to be burnt at the stake; under Elizabeth he hunted Catholics to the death.'

Immortality came also to the twelfth Earl (1752—1834), who launched the first Derby with the result that many thousands of people around the world have much to thank him for. This event came about when Lord Derby took a house called The Oaks at Epsom, outside London, in the heyday of its popularity as a spa. It had been immensely popular since the seventeenth century, when it had become fashionable for over-fed Londoners to allow their over-indulged stomachs and livers the benefit of its waters. Epsom grew and for a time supplanted Tunbridge Wells as the most frequented of spas. Entertainments were provided for the visitors, including races on the Downs and, long after Epsom had had its reversals of fortune, the racing there continued to prosper. But the real turning point in Epsom's otherwise uneventful history came in 1773, when the twelfth Earl had a houseparty at which it was decided to hold a race for three-year-old colts and fillies, its name to be chosen by the toss of a coin. Present was Sir Charles Bunbury, the foremost racing man of the day and contester for the honour of bestowing his name on the new race. Had he won, it would now be called the Bunbury Stakes

Today, the Derby is practically a national day of celebration when even the most timorous, with their once-a-year money, back a horse. 150,000 people attend the Epsom event, which costs £500,000 to stage and a little over £1,250,000 to administer. Nowadays it attracts more than £40 million in bets — oh, and it generates a staggering seventy-five tons of litter. The Derby Stakes has become one of the greatest races of all time (worldwide, there are 300 other Derbys named after it), one that our hero won in 1787 with Sir Peter Teazle, a colt he had bred himself. It was not until 1924, when Sansovino won, that another Earl of Derby, the seventeenth, again carried off the 'Blue Ribbon

of the Turf'. The seventeenth Earl (1865—1948) was none other than the 'King of Lanca-shire', a benevolent personage and formidable figure of the Turf who sported the familiar racing colours of black silks and white cap. He was three times a winner of the Derby (Sansovino having been his first). As an owner and a breeder, he was outstandingly suc-cessful — no other English breeder has exercised a comparable influence on bloodstock breeding throughout the world. He also owned three of the outstanding stallions of modern times — Hyperion, Fairway and Pharos — ensuring that he, too, achieved im-mortality. For, by these and out of various illustrious mares that he also owned were bred great lines of racehorses whose bloodstock survives even now.

Other names are up in lights at the Derby nowadays. Fortunes, and the wherewithal to fund the breeding of racehorses, have shifted since the days when most horses entered in the race were owned by dukes, earls and the richer gentry. The grandees of the Turf in the twentieth century are captains of industry, catfood heiresses, merchants and Arab princes grown rich on the proceeds of oil. Not that the breeding of humankind matters all that much at Epsom. It has long since ceased to be the preserve of the upper classes, and although anybody entering the Epsom Race Club enclosure still wears the obligatory morning dress, it doesn't matter a hoot whether the fortune of the wearer is based on sausage-making or soft porn.

In any case, the merits of being in the Enclosure are arguable. It might relieve the crush out with the herd and, certainly, commands the best view, but frankly the vast majority would prefer to be sitting on the upper deck of a sawn-off double-decker bus strategically placed for maximum viewing, or else wandering about amongst the hot dog stands and the beer tents, placing bets with familiar bookies and generally having as much raucous fun as possible. Anyway, if it's very hot, who wants to be wrapped in woollen morning dress? Out with the rabble, at least those over-heating can resort to their bathing costumes if they so desire. And they do. Bikinis are not unknown at the Derby.

Rabble or royalty, Derby-goers are united by the kicks they get from this most thrill-ing of horse races.

INSIDER TIPS

✦ For those going by car, go as early as possible to avoid traffic jams. The gates open at 10.00a.m.

✦ If you get there early enough, there are plenty of places to park — take your pick.

✦ It is possible to reserve a car parking space in advance — this way you get the closest you can to the racecourse.

✦ Take the usual racing gear with you: binoculars, hipflask, umbrella and/or sun cream, plenty of cash.

TROOPING THE COLOUR

JUNE

'WELCOME TO PERHAPS the most famous parade ground in the world. 7,000 spectators are in their seats, the massed bands and foot guards are in their places, and all is ready . . .'

The reverential tones of the BBC are unchanging. Year after year, for the benefit of radio listeners and television viewers at home and abroad, it delivers a running commentary of summer's Trooping the Colour ceremony, held in honour of the Queen's Official Birthday. The commentator describes events as they unfold, from the moment the first spectators take their seats in Horse Guards Parade to the arrival and subsequent departure of Her Majesty from and to Buckingham Palace.

The commentator's diction is marked by its note of respect, the commentary by its candour and the odd humorous interjection as, say, the behaviour of an unruly horse is remarked upon. Time is marked by descriptions of the uniforms, the minutiae of their detailing, and by anecdotes about the battalions present as well as, of course, the weather. Where would the world be without the BBC informing us about this, the most solemn and majestic of British occasions? Staging it without the BBC would be like holding the ceremony without Her Majesty.

Trooping the Colour is the ceremonial review of part of the Household Division by their Colonel-in-Chief, Her Majesty the Queen. It was first performed on the Sovereign's birthday for King George III and it continued throughout Queen Victoria's long reign, the foot guards performing this same ceremonial parade in honour of her birthday, which was on 24 May. It has continued ever since, held on a day set aside as the Sovereign's Official Birthday.

Like royal weddings and state openings of Parliament, it provides London with its finest hour. There is nothing ersatz about it; this is for real, and it provides links with many scenes and customs of historic interest. No moment in the entire British Season can equal the pageantry and tradition that finds expression as the Queen rides in from the Mall, escorted by a Sovereign's Escort of Household Cavalry, and attended by a royal procession.

As head of the fighting services, the Queen used to ride on ahead of all, just as at the Cenotaph she stands in front, quite alone. The symbolism of this is obvious: this isn't mother and wife but Queen Regnant. After the firing of blanks at her in 1981 by a crazed seventeen-year-old (who was subsequently jailed under the Treason Act 1842), the Queen, who on that occasion was wearing a long navy blue riding-skirt with a military tunic, was escorted by four of the Household Cavalry down the Mall and rode alone only on the parade ground. Now, she goes in an open carriage in a hat and coat, the exigencies of riding side-saddle — at least for Trooping the Colour — a thing of the past. The only time she leaves it is to sit on a small dais marooned in a vast expanse of the parade ground, while the battalions are dragooned in formation backwards and forwards in front of her.

The parade itself is based on the ceremony used for guard mounting in the eighteenth century, when the battalion providing guards for the day trooped the Colour to be carried on the King's Guard. It took place on the great parade ground behind the handsome Horse Guards building, designed in about 1745 by William Kent and erected after his death. This was the new headquarters for the Horse Guards who were the troop, formed in the reign of Charles II for the protection of the King's person, who had stables and barracks in the old Tilt Yard between Whitehall and St James's Park.

The parade ground is still the same, with Admiralty House to the east and the Treasury and Downing Street to the west, though today this ancient site has been relegated to a more ignominious role as a car park for civil servants — their Ford Montegos, however, are booted out when the troops come in. This is the heart of London, and here tradition has preserved the ancient uniform and the duty of keeping watch, though in reality anybody can wander freely from parade ground, under the arch, to Whitehall. On the way, the mounted guards, got up in their exotic bird-of-the-wilds attire — white-plumed helmets, vermilion tunics, white gauntlets and buckskin breeches — are the focus of irreverent spectator sport as Burberry-clad Japanese tourists and Italians in anoraks jostle to have their photographs taken beside them. Here, too, the Changing of the Guard takes place with almost as much pageantry as the Trooping the Colour.

For first-time spectators there is nothing quite like this event, with its massed bands and serried ranks of polished boots marching in time to the music, which normally contains a flavour of the regiment whose Colour is being trooped and which always includes the regimental slow and quick marches for the march past of all regiments on parade. If, unlike those Commonwealth representatives in national dress who can be seen clambering into their numbered places on the tiers erected round three sides of Horse Guards Parade, you haven't got an official seat, you must go quickly to the Mall, or you'll see nothing.

Here and along the rest of the processional route, spectators are grabbing the best viewing positions they can find. Terrible decisions have to be made: do you wait and watch near the palace forecourt, in which case you'd see both departure and return of the royal party but would have a long, long wait in the middle while the Queen is trooping the Colour? Or do you go as near as possible to the parade ground on the edge of St James's Park and try to see the ceremony itself, in which case you risk seeing nothing at all because that's where the crowds are most restricted. Maybe you should run between the two, following the events as they unfold — an idea which would be worth contemplating if only the crowds lining the Mall (ten deep at some points) weren't such an impediment to speed. And now that Her Majesty does the round trip from palace to parade and back in the ivory-mounted phaeton, while not exactly at breakneck speed, her journey is faster than it used to be.

The best advice is to stay on the edge of the Mall under the trees. That way, if the sun is too hot, there is shade. There again, if it rains you have shelter and here, of all the viewing points, you see the procession advancing, passing *and* retreating, the Queen up near the front, Their Royal Highnesses Prince Philip, The Prince of Wales, The Duke of Kent and The Grand Duke of Luxembourg behind her and, bringing up the rear, a gaggle of crown equerries, equerries-in-waiting, grooms, the Silver Stick-in-Waiting, troopers of the Blues and Royals, more grooms and lots more troopers.

To ensure that you discharge your duty as a loyal spectator and manage to see all this pageantry clacking and jingling by on horseback, stake a claim to your post with a folding seat or plant a shooting stick firmly into the ground and cling on to it. Out there, other spectators and royal watchers are equally determined to get the best possible view, and there will be no compunction about seizing yours if your attention is diverted, even for a second. After all, the quarry consist of more than just the Queen. Apart from the bevy of royal dukes accompanying her on the ride down the Mall, there is the Queen Mother whose arrival, preceding the Queen's, is heralded by a barouche driven into Horse Guards Parade where she, like her daughter, is received with a royal salute. Then she vanishes into the comfort of the Horse Guards building to take up her post with other royals and nearly royals, who can be seen looking out of the large window above the central arch at the parade ground below.

Royal watchers are a formidable band amongst whom there exists a solidarity cast in iron. They were out camping in the dewy Mall on the night prior to the first open day of Buckingham Palace, and they see each other at royal weddings and on the Queen Mother's birthday, when she steps out of Clarence House to thank the crowd gathered at

its gates for their birthday greetings. They scan the lists of royal engagements in *The Times* in the hope of finally getting to see an elusive member of The Firm, and sometimes they turn up with a corgi or two at a royal ribbon-cutting. They notch up sightings in little black books, rather like train spotters. If you must, pick one out of the crowd and stick to them like glue because they know all the best viewing spots. Luckily, they are usually recognizable — look for the sleeping bag, the Union Jack and the flask of tea.

By lunch time it's over. The royal procession has vanished beyond the portals of the palace and, concludes the BBC, 'It's time for us to take our leave now, at the end of another triumph of British pageantry majestically performed.'

Royal Ascot

'THE BRITISH CAN organise a succession of glorious traditional summer events with more panache and glamour than any other nation can muster', says the *Daily Telegraph*, heaping praise on the key surviving events of the Season. Goodwood, Wimbledon, Cowes, Royal Ascot — these are all classic examples, but Ascot perhaps, of them all, is the most exceptional.

Its stature in the social calendar approaches the divine: it appeals to international racegoers — the kind who own private planes and studs; it has a certain regal splendour bestowed on it by the patronage of royalty; the local upper crust are there *en masse*, if not racing their own horses then almost certainly reminiscing about the days, now long gone, when they did; the racing itself is of the highest quality, with the best flat races of the season, many of which tend to be championships in their own class. Money, power, influence, dash, glamour — all these are represented in the headiest mixture imaginable. For social aspirants, Royal Ascot is a dream come true.

But for any of this to be of use to the aspirant, he or she must first get beyond the flunkey at the entrance to the Royal Enclosure, currently one Lt.-Col. Sir Piers Bengough, KCVO, OBE, DL, Her Majesty's Representative at Ascot since 1982. The qualifications for entry are much the same as they once were for court presentations and levees and they are still rigorously applied. Sir Piers is the final arbiter of one's eligibility to enter the Royal Enclosure, and to him one must apply months in advance for the privilege of doing so. This is hallowed territory. Here the royals set the tone and up to 7,000 people are allowed in to experience it and to bask in the reflected lustre of the Royal Box which is set slightly apart, festooned with floral tributes.

HM's Representative will require the signature of a sponsor who has been granted vouchers for the enclosure on at least eight previous, preferably recent, occasions before even considering you. Until just a few years ago, you were refused entry for being divorced. If you're personally known to him there shouldn't be too much of a problem getting in, but if you're the wrong sort of person well, all that awaits you is a space amongst 'the rest' in the Grandstand (£12), or the Silver Ring (£2.50), or the Heath (£1.00).

Happily, wherever you happen to find yourself, Ascot is as fashionable and as popular now as it was in the eighteenth century, when one correspondent wrote, 'In place of a Grand Stand stood a row of some thirty to forty towering booths, in which were gathered the flower of English nobility, beauties of the first distinction, and the most celebrated personages in the Kingdom, together with the pickpockets, sporting blacklegs, and well-known sharks that added a spice of risk and adventure to the proceedings.'

For the uninitiated, Royal Ascot is a goldfish bowl in which to observe closely the madness and excesses of the British class system in action. Here the social pyramid — Queen at the pinnacle, peasants down below and, in the middle, the Royal Enclosure full of Jockey Club grandees, blue bloods, film stars, social aspirants who've made it — is stripped bare for all to study. And you don't even have to be in the Royal Enclosure to watch it run its dotty course throughout the four days of the Ascot race meeting: simply come armed with binoculars and a ticket to the Grandstand and Paddock and look over the fence. There you have it: all the women will be wearing hats — because Sir Piers won't let them in without one — with day dresses, and the men decked out in morning or service dress.

Ascot is one of the few seasonal opportunities for everyone to be a peacock — though acceptability in the presence of royalty requires that you are the right sort of peacock, a deterrent against over-theatrical sartorial displays that seems to be only half-heartedly applied. For years it has allowed through its net the eccentric Mrs Schilling in ever larger and more outrageous hats and, in 1993, a girl dressed from head to toe in Astroturf. Said one aristocratic young woman going through her dizzy period: 'It seems crazy spending heaps of money on an outfit that's just going to get soaked at Ascot. But I love dressing up — that's the joy of the Season. I just wish the men could find a way of jazzing up all that grey without having to invest in those terrible flowery waistcoats' (*Tatler*, 1992).

Spurred on by the example of the Royal Enclosure, those outside it are dressed to the nines also. This increases the frivolity of the event, making it into an 'occasion' long awaited, much enjoyed on the day and sorely missed when over. But fashion editors are

RACE CARD £1

constantly haranguing their readers about their dress sense on occasions like Ascot —
whether destined for the Royal Enclosure or not. Indeed, they are full of what Lady This
or That wore — never mind what the horses were up to. In the *Daily Telegraph*: 'Why the
British woman is a non-starter at Ascot . . . how not to dress.' Others laud our ladies:
'Mrs Guy Sangster showed a new way with short in a fit-and-flare lace dress by Bruce
Oldfield.' Some racegoers maintain that you only notice the people at Ascot who are
badly or outrageously dressed. Not so. Mrs Sangster looked fabulous; so did Mrs Steven
Harris in her Philip Treacy 'saucer' hat and cats'-eyes sunglasses.

Her Majesty the Queen doesn't notice what anybody else is wearing. She arrives in a
kind of fashion parade all of her own, the outriders on her landau got up in scarlet coats
and gold-laced hats, the postilions in purple, red and gold. Like her predecessor Queen
Anne who, whatever her other virtues, is remembered in Turf lore chiefly for having
founded Royal Ascot, Her Majesty is nuts about racing, frequently entering competitions
with her own horses. Few other monarchs, certainly no other female ones, have had as
dedicated an affinity with the Turf as Queens Anne and Elizabeth II. A frequent visitor to
the racing at Newmarket and York, Queen Anne is supposed to have allowed her beady
eye to alight on Ascot Common in 1711 and, it being a sportsmanlike eye, noticed the

natural advantages that it offered for her favourite sport. Thus Ascot came into being.

The first meeting was held in August 1711, the Queen having ridden over from Windsor Forest to inaugurate The Ascot Races in a 'brilliant suite' containing the sensation of the day, the beautiful Miss Forester, maid-of-honour, mounted and dressed like a man in a 'long white riding coat, full-flapped waistcoat, court hat bound with gold (point to the front), and a flowing periwig'. Thus attired, the elegant Miss Forester drew attention away from the monarch, perhaps heralding modern Ascot's most newsworthy attribute (after the horses). Her Majesty presented her own Plate worth 100 guineas, 'to be run for', according to the *London Gazette* of 12 July 1711, 'round the new beat at Ascot Common, near Windsor, on Tuesday, August 7th next, by any horse, mare or gelding, being no more than 6 years old the grass before, as must be certified under the hand of the breeder, carrying 12 st., 3 heats, to be entered the last day of July, at Mr Hancock's, at Fernhill, near the starting post'. So pleased was Anne that she attended another gathering on the Common in September of the same year.

Unsurprisingly, Ascot prospered, though royal patronage waxed and waned with successive generations of kings and queens. George I wasn't particularly interested, neither was George II. It was not until the reign of George III that the meeting gave its first indications of being likely to become one of the foremost in the country, and by 1777 it was being described as 'Windsor and Ascot Heath Races'. In that season, a Cup race was instituted over a four-mile course, resulting in a walkover in its inaugural year. This was the origin of the Ascot Gold Cup, a race which has since become one of the greatest in the annals of the Turf.

But for all the hype and the razzle-dazzle, it's the jockeys and the horses on which any race meeting depends for a good day's entertainment, as Fitzstephen, chronicler in the age of Henry II, has recorded: 'The horses on their part are not without emulation; they tremble and are impatient and are continually in motion. At last, the signal once given, they strike, devour the course, hurrying along with unremitting velocity. The jockeys, inspired with the thought of applause and the hopes of victory, clap spurs to their willing horses, brandish their whips, and cheer them with their cries.'

INSIDER TIPS

✦ Royal Ascot, like most events in or near to London, is marred by traffic jams. If there is a means of getting there other than by car, take it.

✦ Picnics are fun — if the sun shines. If it threatens not to, then take rolls of plastic sheeting, totally unchic, yes, but eminently practical. Reserve a car parking spot in advance.

✦ Get yourself invited to a decent picnic, or to a lunch in one of the corporate boxes.

✦ Forget the dress code at your peril; check with the Ascot Office if you're not sure.

✦ Remember to take a raincoat, an umbrella and the binoculars.

THE ALL ENGLAND LAWN TENNIS
CHAMPIONSHIPS, WIMBLEDON

THERE ARE PLENTY of tennis heroes in the Pantheon of the Gods. They are modern heroes — stars, champions and, these days, multimillionaires. Their turn to burnish their laurels comes annually in June, at The All England Lawn Tennis Championships at Wimbledon, slap in the middle of the British Sporting Season.

Society is present, though hereditary grandees are a bit thin on the ground. For it is the aristocracy of Pop and Celluloid who have colonized the Season's tennis event, with a supporting cast of more ordinary mortals distinguished not by their social class but by an enthusiasm for the game. This point is made to admirable effect when, at the appointed hour, the spectators stream into the grounds, a mass of sun visors, panamas and straw bonnets, all LA beachwear and bank holiday Monday at Margate. Film stars are treated with more deference than the duchess of ancient lineage and princesses behave like film stars. Even the Archbishop of Canterbury lets go a little. It might be said that Wimbledon, finally, is truly classless.

Make no mistake though, tennis at Wimbledon is still an august institution, if for different reasons than in the past. For, alone of all the events of the British Season, this championship yields an international glamour to those who take part, whether in the spectator's seat or on the 'stage'. Both are participants of a great modern drama which is beamed into 600 million homes around the globe.

From Maud Watson, Wimbledon's first home-grown female champion, to the great Suzanne Lenglen, the first superstar in her field and seven times a winner, to the glittering array of latter-day deities — Bjorn Borg, Billie Jean King, Martina Navratilova, Boris Becker and Steffi Graf are just a few beacons of tennis brilliance — Centre Court at Wimbledon has always been the Olympus of their endeavour. Why else would spectators without a seat be allowed to pass through its hallowed portals before play begins just to photograph it — empty?

There is a peculiar drama and ritual attendant on sporting arenas, none more so nowadays than the tennis courts at Wimbledon. Here, annually at The All England Lawn Tennis Championships, victim after victim is lead, lamb-like, to the slaughter, to pit

strength and skill, courage and grace against another under pressure, knowing that the rewards if they win are immense.

The higher the stakes, the greater the drama – as it was in the world's most famous arena, the ancient Colosseum in Rome. Even Sue Barker, former world Number 3, couldn't curtsey to the Royal Box before game commenced because her knees, a-tremble, wouldn't bend. White-knuckle angst also reaches the spectators and is etched on their faces, royal princesses, film stars and ordinary mortals alike. In deadpan staccato the umpire proclaims, 'Match point.' A deafening silence falls like a mantle over the Club. The nail-biting stops and there is no movement in the crowded ranks of the auditorium but the left-to-right swivelling of hundreds of pairs of eyes. The only sounds are ball-on-racket-on-court until, when the fate of the players is sealed, the crowd erupts in a frenzy of jubilation. Sport's insatiable appetite has been fed another champion.

But the loser? In 1993 a bitterly disappointed Jana Novotna wept miserably on the shoulder of a kindly royal duchess when she lost the Women's Final to Steffi Graf,

the blow doubly hard since victory had seemed imminent. Instead, Graf accepted the gift of her opponent's errors, thumping a winning smash past the dejected Novotna before running into the crowd to hug the euphoric members of her support group. Her reward? A princely cheque and additional bolstering of her exalted position, now the five-times winner of Wimbledon's famous silver-gilt plate.

But even the loser can expect some bounty, magnanimously granted because he or she proved themselves able enough to play on this hallowed ground. No such reward for the runners-up in ancient Rome. Losers at gladiatorial battles or Christians faced by wild beasts, far from being able

to sink into the comforting open arms of a royal personage, expected to emerge from 'play' as an ignominious heap of dead flesh, mauled and limbless.

But tennis at Wimbledon wasn't always like this. Although enthusiasm for it in the past was every bit as keen as it is today, The All England Lawn Tennis Championships was once just another event on the calendar of the London Season to which you went in a certain style in June, after the Eton–Harrow cricket match at Lord's and before the Cowes Regatta. For the ladies, it was hats and gloves; for the men a collar and tie. Both were the epitome of decorum — after all, a royal patron was present. Even now, the last vestige of Wimbledon's status as a Society event is the royal patronage it continues to enjoy, the Duchess of Kent having made the tournament her charge just as Ascot is the Queen's. And female players, no matter what their origin, still acknowledge her presence with a curtsey.

It was a gentler spectacle until the fashion-conscious Lenglen was unleashed on Wimbledon, her leaping flight to the ball a personal ballet which helped throw off the shackles of the corset. In her wake, dress designer Ted Tinling eased women players out of their 'armour' and into short dresses and frilly knickers — a departure from the sartorial norm that brought with it a lot of naked calf and thigh. The stakes were raised as women proved that they, too, could earn big money. Tennis and Wimbledon have never been the same since.

And yet, for all the dash and glamour of super-tennis, to the British the sounds of the court — the thwack of ball on racket, the sharp expulsion of air by players as they serve — are the unmistakeable signs of summer. Beyond the razzmatazz, they hint at something more benign and, appropriately, the appearance of Wimbledon's tennis club is

modelled on an Edwardian country house garden, its tournament reminiscent of a village summer fête.

Amongst plump picnic lawns, neatly shorn hedges and trim wooden fences, the court buildings are buried deep within tangles of ivy and climbing roses. If there was a gardener, she'd be patrician, all straw hat and pearls. There is cream with strawberries — twenty-three tons of them. It's all *so* English that 370,000 enthusiasts wolf down 190,000 little sandwiches and 80,000 half pints of Pimms, while the 12,500 bottles of champagne consumed conjure up some of the frivolity of Society at a social beano in the 1920s.

This is a sophisticated artifice and it belies the cut-and-thrust of today's international game. The rustic folly in the corner conceals fax machines and merchandising contracts for successful players, and the arbour by the gate is, in reality, the home of the programme vendor. But none of this is really the point. What matters is the parochial atmosphere of an older, other England which provides a counterpoint to the raw commerciality attendant on any international sporting tournament. After all, this is a club with a queen for a patron and there are certain rules of play, dress and behaviour. This is the humanizing element. Even the players admit it attracts them: Navratilova began her love affair with the All England Club or, more specifically, its traditions and its 'classiness', as she once described it, in 1973. She had a point. This is Wimbledon's appeal. 'It *is* tennis', she once said.

It helps, of course, that Wimbledon proper views itself as a village to whose teashops, pubs and high street an olde worlde persona attaches. Perhaps this also attracts the players who like to rent its homes from inhabitants who move out for the duration of the tournament. And then there is the vast and precious greenery of the adjacent Common — all 1,100 acres of it — preserving intact, far from the reality of the countryside, the rural idyll which is so crucial to the wellbeing of all Londoners. Even its trees against a thundercloud are pure Constable. At its edge, The All England Lawn Tennis & Croquet Club straddles a hill from which, in the distance, the tall spire of St Mary's and the sylvan glades of the Common can be seen. This is Arcadia and at its core lies the essence of the British Season.

INSIDER TIPS

❧ Leave your car at home unless you like traffic jams and expensive parking charges. Wimbledon is very easily reached by public transport from the centre of London.

❧ Tickets for Centre and No. I Courts are like gold dust. To get one you must apply via the public ballot (see page 124 for details).

❧ If all else fails, you can still get into Wimbledon by queuing at the gate at midday — admission is £7 in the first week and £6 in the second. These tickets give access to the outside courts and can be used for standing room in the show courts. After 5.00p.m. admission price is reduced.

❧ 2,000 tickets are available on the middle Saturday on a first-come-first-served basis. For the best seats, queue on the Friday before.

❧ If it's hot, take a sunhat and sunblock cream. Temperatures have been known to reach 45°C (120°F).

THE HENLEY ROYAL REGATTA

THERE IS ONE major difference between the original regatta which took place at Henley in 1839 and the event you will have read about in the papers in the summer of 1993. Women were present. And not just in large hats. The same, magnificent stretch of the River Thames was — and probably always will be — used for the event's racing and the weather was gloriously hot. The sport was as competitive as ever and changes, where they took place, were mostly only marginal. Even the races, originally controlled from horseback on the towpath, are still controlled from launches built nowadays in the same mould as the first steam launch commissioned for this purpose in 1874 — a generation of grandfathers would no doubt recognize them today. But dramatically and without precedent, women were allowed to compete in the full course of the regatta for the first time in the 154-year history of the event.

Women have rowed at Henley before, of course, but *only* at invitation events over a short course in the 1980s. In 1993, however, they were allowed to compete in the single sculls events for the first time. Previously, the excuses that the gentlemen of Henley's management committee usually came up with in their efforts to deter women from joining in, and to divert attention from this extraordinary anomaly, ranged from the standard of women's rowing being insufficiently high, to five days not being long enough to include it. Women were — and probably still are — deemed simply not good enough to compete in this staunchly male-only celebration of endurance and strength, in spite of the fact that at least one of the competitors in the 1993 events was an Olympic gold medallist. Ironically, women at Henley are not even competing against the men, just keeping to their own events.

Until this astonishing about-turn, Henley with women was a bit like Wimbledon without them — unimaginable. Women rowers have the inclusion of a World Cup event in the regatta to thank for this (since women take part in World Cup rowing, there was no way that Henley could lock them out) and the stuffed shirts have been well and truly beaten — for the moment. But nobody yet knows whether 1993 was just a one-off. Only time will tell.

Boating has always been a way of life at Henley-on-Thames, a sunny Oxfordshire town straddling the river just thirty-six miles from London. It is the kind of place tourists hunt out for the views: here riverside, swans, church tower, eighteenth-century inns — one of them inevitably the Red Lion Hotel — and background vistas of wooded hills, unite in evocation of an older England slumbering peacefully, unaware of the chaos of the modern world. But the regatta is chiefly the reason that Henley is a household word — even in America. Royalty, in the form of Prince Albert in 1851, bestowed its favour on the event, a milestone in the history of Henley that was soon followed, in 1887, by a visit from the Prince of Wales, the future Edward VII. The present Queen isn't interested in boats, though Prince Andrew did present the prizes in 1985.

The most prominent rowing club competing in the event is Leander, membership of which gives the rower the right to wear salmon pink socks and tie. Not everyone's version of chic, but it gains the wearer and his guests, male and female, entry to one or two exclusive zones on the river bank during regatta week, thus uniting the rowing buffs and the socialites. Year after year, Leander's teams are rather conspicuous as they win races, break records and haul in the trophies; a few of its members have earned their Olympic laurels, and from its ranks come most of the regatta's stewards.

There are three ways of looking at the regatta: as the premier rowing event of the year, one widely respected internationally and competed in by international teams; as an all-male preserve into which women are 'invited' under sufferance and on condition they disport themselves according to archaic rules imposed on them by the (male) governors of the event; as a jolly summertime knees-up on the riverside, one on to which the old divisions of society are superficially imposed by the exclusion of non-members from club enclosures which, in turn, have their own hierarchies distinguishing best from indifferent.

That the regatta is the premier rowing event of the year there is no doubt; records are frequently beaten and form books upset as first-class racing by world champions, not all of them British, demolish the opposition. And yet, for all this and in spite of the fact that some of the teams contain, say, world junior, or lightweight, gold and silver medallists,

the regatta remains one of the true bastions of amateur sport. It is entirely non-commercial. There is no sponsorship and no advertising, and the rules and regulations governing it are laid out by the Stewards of Henley Royal Regatta, a fierce oligarchy whose decisions are maddeningly eccentric though nonetheless governed by an impeccable sense of fair play. Above all, though, it keeps up with changes in the sport.

Oarsmen from all over the world descend on Henley to compete in its races — even though the extent of the river set aside for the racing is way out of scale with any Olympic venue. Here, there is only space for two teams to race abreast; a course of Olympic proportions requires several teams to be able to race together. Russian crews come, so do Canadian, South African and American, each competing for a variety of trophies, like the Grand Challenge Cup (which dates from 1839), the Ladies Challenge Plate (for all-male teams not quite up to the standard of the former), the Thames Challenge Cup (for smaller clubs and single college boat clubs), the prestigious Diamond Sculls trophy (instituted in 1850 for single oarsmen), the Silver Goblet for the Pair-Oared Race, and the Princess Elizabeth Cup for schools — opened to overseas crews in the early 1960s.

As with any competition, there are bound to be disappointments. But perhaps the most depressing of all, in the most recent regatta, was the fate of the South African team from Selbourne College. The eight, having travelled 6,000 miles at vast expense to race in the Princess Elizabeth Cup, raced less than 100 metres before their number four's seat disintegrated. Henley does not have a 100 metre rule such as that which operates in true international regattas under FISA regulations, allowing a race to be stopped and re-rowed in the event of equipment failure before the mark. The hapless South African boys could only paddle in with their numbers three and four immobilized.

Others face different hazards. Collision is one of them: rowers with the opposition, or rowers with the photographers' box. And occasionally the cox will forget to carry the makeweights to bring his own weight up to the minimum for coxes. This happened in the 1993 Temple Challenge Cup and the regatta, under new management for the first time in fifteen years, underlined the fact that little has changed by dealing with this problem in a characteristically idiosyncratic way. The stewards decided that the missing

weight had not affected the outcome of the race and awarded the offenders one 'false start' to carry into the next round. It is probably true that the missing weight, equivalent to a pair of training shoes, was insignificant, but the ruling may be misinterpreted in the future.

The second version of Henley is true if you're a man and a member of one of the leading clubs, preferably Leander, or you have the right to enter the Stewards' Enclosure. The ugly picture of man's inhumanity to female rowers has already been portrayed. But what about their female guests? These are pre-eminent over their sisters in the sculls only if their knees are covered and they don't wear culottes or trousers, draconian rules which female participants, in the unofficial uniform of lycra shorts and T-shirts, prefer to circumvent by staying close to the boat tent. Anyone defying the rule is barred entry to the enclosure. The line of thought giving rise to these absurd ideas is as befuddled as that which keeps women out of gentlemen's clubs and which makes the English — grown men in particular — defer to Nanny. Women are tolerated but only in a supporting role. They must be either servile or decorative, but never equal. This concept derives from some antique notion about male supremacy, ossified deep in a nostalgia for the past and reverence for tradition. Only the inclusion of a World Cup event cracked it, allowing the participation of women in 1993. However, nothing short of an Amazonian revolution is going to lift those hemlines.

Thus, decorum established unto the whims of Henley's oligarchical tyrants, the party begins. This, the third view of Henley, is the other life of the regatta and for some the only view of it. There are house parties and picnics out in the car park — not any old bit of empty space in which vehicles are deposited, but the one for which you pay a fee in advance, thus ensuring yourself of a position next to last year's neighbours. There, you unload the hampers, the fizzy drinks and the Pimms, the contents of the picnic, the garnishes and the sauces inspired by an abundance of 'summer season' food articles flourishing in the colour supplements at this time of year.

But the party really begins when the straw hats and the boaters, the gaudy club ties, and white flannels and blazers are fished out of mothballs the morning before. There is an evocation of yesteryear which, in its innocence, is slightly unreal: nothing is odder than dreary Paddington Station over Henley weekend — the important 'social' Saturday and Sunday — packed with regatta-goers incongruous amongst the backpackers and suitcases bound for the West Country and Wales. Nobody knows whether to laugh in derision or draw breath in awe at this spectacle trailing decoratively by on its way to catch the Henley Express.

This fancy-dress 'apartheid' is one of the strangest aspects of the British Season, perhaps the cause of its frivolity and the reason for its endurance even through the social upheavals that came in the wake of two world wars. But for all its peculiarities, Henley without a dress code would be too ordinary. It might even be boring. Dressing up to play is an amusing diversion. The British Season would be the worse off without it.

INSIDER TIPS

⚓ Women: remember the dress code if you are to be a guest in the Stewards' Enclosure. It's not much fun sitting outside while your friends are having fun within. Hats are only necessary if you want to avoid being sunburnt.

⚓ Men: take a tie. You never know when you might need it.

⚓ Everybody: the weather over the 1993 regatta weekend was very hot indeed. Take sunblock or do as the beauty editors tell you and anoint yourselves with high factor suncream.

⚓ British Rail puts on an extra service to Henley from London's Paddington Station during the regatta. Use it. The traffic jams down the M4 and the A423 near Maidenhead are an irritating waste of precious regatta time.

⚓ Private picnics are better value than anything on sale at the regatta. Let's face it, they avoid having to fight through the scrum for overpriced prawns and warm champagne on sale there. If you come by car, do the whole picnic thing in the car park: chairs, linen, crystal, silver (butler).

INTERNATIONAL CRICKET, LORD'S

SMART PEOPLE, SO they say, listen to test cricket on the radio while watching the picture on TV. Others consider it even better, and infinitely more challenging, to listen to both commentaries at the same time. But people who do either of these are deluding themselves and wasting an opportunity to see in the flesh what Michael Parkinson calls a 'unique, very psychological, physical, complex, beautiful game, aesthetically and hugely pleasing'. These and other superlatives apply if the venue is the Marylebone Cricket Club (the MCC or Lord's), the world's cricket headquarters.

For one thing, cricket at Lord's, particularly for spectators *in situ* there, is likely to be amongst the best of matches anywhere. It has been since the club came into being in 1787, playing its first game a year later against the club which spawned it — the White Conduit Club, which was founded in 1752. It sets the rules and is a byword for fair play. Certainly, the 'cricket experience' — the sun on neck as you watch cream-clad figures darting about an emerald green pitch, the intermittent dull clack of ball-on-bat accompaniment, the 'howzat' appeal to the spectator, the poses, the nostalgia and the chauvinism, the picnics and the gin and tonics, the setting (redolent of an older pastoral England of matches on village greens and country house lawns), the formal informality requiring members to wear the psychedelic club tie yet allowing them also to be in shirt sleeves, not to mention the high-strung emotions attendant on any world class sporting competition — is unmissable. It is also hugely beguiling if you're a first-timer.

This is the special appeal of Lord's. 'Cricket,' says Anne Boston in the *Observer*, 'represents in its most extreme form the Englishman's capacity for self-delusion and his desire to present himself as he would like to be seen, rather than how he really is.' It doesn't really matter, to the observer at any rate, whether the English teams win or lose. Says Boston, 'It's the ritual that counts, and the clothes and the whole code.' And while the game may not be what it was, the punters will never tire of lazing the summer's day away, lounging somewhere congenial, sunhat on head, with match — any match — in motion on the pitch.

Often there is, of course, vicious competition: in particular, the international test

matches, which incite jubilation, humiliation and embarrassment to equal degree. The first Lord's Test, and the fifteenth between England and Australia, was held there in 1884. England was the winner. By that time, cricket had only been played on these grounds for seventy years (since they had been taken over in 1814, nine years after the first Eton *v.* Harrow match was played). At one time, this last match *was* 'Lord's' and was played in July during Long Leave. From it, it was expected future cricket heroes would emerge. Some did. Until the First World War, those matches attracted Society: as a key sporting element of the London Season, it was one of the events you went to automatically, along with the Derby, Ascot and Goodwood, Wimbledon, the Henley Regatta and Cowes. The standard of the cricket was high and playing at Lord's was, as it is today, considered by those who've done it as the highest achievement of their lives.

While the Eton *v.* Harrow match is still played today, the international test matches have eclipsed it. Sadly though, England have not beaten Australia at Lord's since Hedley Verity's match in 1934. Then, heavy rain affected the pitch, uncovered in those days, and Verity, the Yorkshire slow left-arm bowler, used it to devastating effect, taking fourteen wickets in the day, including six in the last hour as England won by an innings and thirty-eight runs. In recent years, the England team has been anything but triumphant. In fact in 1993, the newspapers were filled with laments for Lord's lost glory. Year after year, this sacred green turf has been the scene of other people's — usually Australia's (they have lost to England in a test match at Lord's only once this century) — latest triumphs. So revered is the venue that it seems to inspire visiting teams, making England's task of winning all the harder.

There is nothing quite like going to Lord's for a test match — for both player and spectator. Lord's has an atmosphere all of its own. John Woodcock, writing in *The Times*, says, 'Australians think of Sydney and

Melbourne, and of course they're right. But Slater, an Aussie from Wagga (a township on the Murrumbidgee River west of Canberra in New South Wales), may never again feel the same exultation, the same feeling of being only a little lower than the angels, as he did when he reached his 100 at Lord's on Tuesday.'

Cricket, whatever the venue, is intoxicating, particularly to the English male. Even Mr Major wilts when another important match is lost, and did you know that John Paul Getty Jnr was introduced to cricket by none other than Mick Jagger? Even the cricket ghosts are all men — and there are plenty of them, whom one can imagine playing cricket silently together on warm summer nights, W. G. Grace and Hedley Verity included. Cricket's HQ is all-male territory, the preserve of the kind of Englishman who loves to wear a uniform — in this case, club tie, navy blazer, neat stone-coloured trousers and, occasionally, a panama hat. Women scarcely feature; the Lord's Pavilion excludes all women except for the Queen and those females there to serve. Is this what the upper classes like to do best, or has it simply got something to do with male superiority?

Nobody really seems to want to address this tricky question, least of all the groups of pink-faced men lying about on picnic rugs on the Pavilion lawns amongst popping corks and the clink of glass and cutlery. The MCC still has to confront properly 'the problem' of admitting women through the hallowed portals of its clubhouse. Sandra Barwick, reporting for the *Independent*, prodded two MCC spectators at a recent test match and asked for their views. Said one: 'Hopefully, they [women] will never be allowed . . . I love my wife dearly, but I don't want her in the Pavilion when I'm watching cricket.' Said the other: 'It's not chauvinism. It's a love of cricket. I don't want to join the Women's Institute.' And so on.

Whether the spectators love the skills involved or are attracted by the variety, or simply by the way that cricket absorbs the individual contribution into the team effort, this is a perverse anachronism and in the last years of the twentieth century it threatens to belittle the traditions of Lord's. It won't change the cricket though; while in most things they generally move with the times at Lord's, this is the one thing that will always remain the same. It represents Englishness. How can it change?

INSIDER TIPS

● If you're bringing a picnic, bring a rug to stake out your territory on the lawn while you go off to watch the match.

● Arrive early to grab a seat (bring a cushion) and perhaps give yourself time also to look around the museum at Lord's.

● With lunch, remember the icebox, the papers or a book.

● Like all other London-based events, it is better to leave the car behind and use public transport. There is nowhere to park.

● A radio with earphones is a good idea — that way, you hear the commentary and see the action in the flesh.

THE ROYAL WELSH SHOW
SIOE FRENHINOL CYMRU — BUILTH WELLS

JULY

IT MIGHT HAVE been The Royal Welsh Show that Thomas Hardy had under scrutiny when he wrote about fair day in *The Mayor of Casterbridge*. 'The trusser and his family . . . soon entered the Fair-field, which showed standing-places and pens . . . the crowd was denser now . . . the frivolous contingent of visitors, including journeymen out for a holiday, a stray soldier or two . . . village shopkeepers, and the like, having latterly flocked in; persons whose activities found a congenial field among the peepshows, toystands, waxworks, inspired monsters . . . thimble-riggers, nick-nack vendors and readers of Fate.' Although the Royal Welsh Show is an agricultural show and Hardy's a livestock auction, the similarities between them are striking. Principally though, both signify freedom from the hard slog of life on the farm, the longed-for summer hiatus in the tough routine before the onslaught of another leaden winter.

Annually, in the third week of July, about 200,000 people and 5,000 head of livestock descend on Builth Wells in Wales. They come in vans, Landrovers and trailers, horse boxes and assorted souped-up Fords, Volvo Estates and caravans — their destination The Royal Welsh Show. Since all accommodation is reserved long before the event, the town billets a stream of caravans and mobile homes, adorned with washing lines and pot plants, deckchairs and barbecues, on the neighbouring hillsides for the duration — a week, sometimes longer. This is the seaside holiday many of the participants never had and here, at landlocked Builth Wells, they are determined to enjoy themselves, rain or shine.

Builth Wells is a small, stone-built town lodged in a cleft in eastern Wales's handsome Black Hills. The natives call it Llanfair Ym Muallt, and it is an unremarkable sort of place, which lived from the tourist trade in the nineteenth century and lives from its market today. It has a church whose origins are Norman, and the remains of a castle whose defences were razed in 1260 by Llewelyn ap Gruffydd, the opponent of Edward I, who was slain nearby in 1282. Its showground at Llanelwedd is the seat of The Royal Welsh Show, the main agricultural event in the Welsh calendar. Its sheds and corrals house a huge range of activities, focusing on the whole of farming and rural life in the region.

Bizarrely, the show has one distinct similarity with those other *fêtes-champêtres* of the British Season: at its heart it is a reflection of an older order. Just as Ascot or Cowes echo the social hierarchy of another age and try desperately to preserve and fortify it as it teeters in and out of fashion, so The Royal Welsh Show indicates a yearning for a traditional way of life fixed in old country customs, rituals and speech — a life before the convulsive transformations of the Industrial Revolution. Without being sentimental, the show, intent on illustrating the rural life as essentially a good life, is an essential feature of summertime for the farming fraternity who exhibit here, as well as for its visitors.

With ebullient optimism, it shows how to make the most of the land, what to take from it and, most important, what to put back in return. Like any other rural fair — and there are plenty of them scattered about the British Isles — it illustrates the art of the countryside and the half-hidden triumphs of farming. In the sunshine, it eulogizes this idyll, providing the farming fraternity with a belief in its activities.

There are fence-making demonstrations, sheepdog trials and horse-shoeing competitions. There are blacksmiths and sheepshearers who yank their charges from the pen, tip them upside down and strip them in front of a cheering audience, the winner being the man who does six quickest. There are produce stalls selling Welsh cakes and Tregroes waffles, Victoria Sponges and elderflower cordials. The Countryside Council for Wales is there, so is the Farming and Wildlife Group, the National Trust and Royal Mail. And while the Clean and Tidy Farm Competition produces a winner each year, it's the livestock that are the most popular and enduring symbols of expert husbandry. Cattle, sheep, pigs, goats and poultry are poked and prodded by the judges, the best specimens turned into champions and led triumphantly around a well-manicured parade ground.

The pedigree Hereford and Limousin bulls turn most heads. Supremely dignified, these huge, vigorous beasts are venerated above all others. Their pedigree and descent, and that of their cows, from admired winners of past shows, are proclaimed on notices pinned to the sides of their stalls: who else would Rousham May be descended from but Rousham Hercules and Essex Emily? Rousham May, however, has nothing on a Longhorn called Dolly, resplendent in her stall with '36' stamped on to the left cheek of her

majestic rump. These are the upper crust of the cattle class and if they were humans they'd live in Belgravia. As it is, they're primped and shampooed, the cows with talcum powder on their udders, the bulls their tails backcombed and blow-dried. Never has muck been kept at bay so well as it is here amongst the prizewinners and their brood.

In a different shed, vast porkers are slumbering or snuffling about quietly — Black Berkshires, the Pink Welsh, and the Oxford Sandy and Black — some with piglets. Here

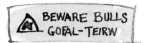

is Lord Emsworth's Empress Blandings and her sisters, Goldfoot Lucky Girl, Gorfelyn Clarissa III and Elspeth, in all their majesty. Then there are the prize sheep, confined to quarters behind wattle fences over which old gents in mud-coloured tweeds lean, each with a cleft stick, muttering to each other in Welsh, all the time picking at a sheep's fleece or peering with quiet concentration at bovine teeth and assessing the result. There are Bleu du Maine with their bluish-grey faces and legs, Berrichon du Cher, Rouge de L'Ouest — each one seems a foreigner until you stumble on the Exmoor Horns, the Welsh Hill Speckled Faces and the Hampshire Downs, the latter silly woolly blobs whose piercing black eyes stare vacantly into space. These were Little Bo-Peep's companions. But while the Hampshires haven't changed, Bo-Peep has — there are no gingham dresses in sight, no lacy caps and certainly no ribbon-tied shoes. That idyll has long departed and modern Bo is a strapping wench, all jeans, cheery smile and great boots, whose task it is to flush out the droppings which threaten to sully the pristine straw and ruin the effects of the shampoo and set of the Hampshires' bouffant fleeces. A product of the nearby Black Hills, modern Bo and her farmer companions have a matter-of-fact attitude to the world, one that can lodge prizewinning ewes and rams beside the refrigeration chamber containing the carcasses of their relatives, sliced clean in two in order that you might judge the inside in addition to the much-lauded outside. To have to wait until you're dead and turned into chops to achieve champion status seems a bit much even for sheep, but they're there lest we forget that these beasts are not only breeders but lunch and dinner also. Another shed sells rack of lamb, joints for the Sunday roast and endless other favourites, from sausages to meatballs and black pudding.

But like Hardy's fair day, The Royal Welsh Show has another life. Away from the serious business of judging, a noisy, seething mass of people swarms around the side attractions. There are booths selling avocado rejuvenating cream, and others where you can buy those pans with 'magic' wipe-clean abilities; nobody is fooled, least of all those whose staple diet — the high cholesterol drama of black pudding, fried eggs and bread, sausage and baked beans — would benefit from an implement such as this. There are craft stands and jacuzzi salesmen, dealers in garden furniture and miniature conifers.

A man demonstrates how to make sausages the easy way, and deftly offloads the new appliance by the cartload. Across the way, a burger bar abuts the purveyor of furry winter hats and bathes them in clouds of greasy smoke, while further on an awning houses rustic types in sandals struggling to demonstrate to a disinterested populace the art of caning chairs. It's not a dying art, but more interesting for the pot-bellied farmhands are the smoky beer tents, which are crammed to overflowing. Two drunks struggle in a heap near the entrance to a shed, inside which homemaking skills are demonstrated to an eager flock of parish wives. At the flower arranging demonstrations — 'every hour, on the hour' — they learn what to do with gladioli and pampas grass, and there is a popular, cut-price clothing stall, interesting because the style of its merchandise went out with the Ark and is making a comeback, and there are bargains to be had.

The alleyways between the stalls and the stands are teeming with life and filled with smells of pot-pourri and burgers, and the babble arising from them is a mixture of English and Welsh. Occasionally, patrician-sounding vowels rise above the mêlée but are soon drowned out by more guttural sounds; Welsh salt-of-the-earth has a more resonant pitch than twinset-and-pearls. Cash registers squeak and, overhead, an aeroplane drones round and round, trailing behind it a sign advertising a new brand of fertilizer. Pushing through the throng, corpulent country matrons of the Ma Larkin genre are making stately progress, their overloaded prams creaking and shaking as they go. They stop only to allow a passing bull, led by a farmhand, more space to deposit a dollop of dung, and to watch while its rear end is deftly spruced up with a clutch of straw, a sage nod all round indicating that this performance would have been given high marks out of ten had there been the judge in attendance.

The Royal Welsh Show is an earthy, gutsy event, a far cry from the blue blazer and Buck's Fizz brigade back in the home counties. One thing unites them all, though: the socializing. Even though the agricultural variety revolves around, say, comparisons of notes on deworming, while get-togethers of different breed societies cement relations and act as channels for gossip and information, this is still networking. And even if you win no prizes, it is a good enough reason for going.

INTERNATIONAL POLO, WINDSOR

JULY

POLO LOOKS EASY enough. On a sunny July day at the Guards Polo Club at Smith's Lawn, surrounded by the old trees of Windsor Great Park, the castle itself a distant speck, it is also remarkably picturesque. There is dash and glamour, too. The handsome players in white breeches and leather boots dart effortlessly, or so it seems, about a brilliant green field on ponies in a flurry of mallets and stampedes, aiming to knock a little four and a half ounce white ball between the goalposts. If someone gets bumped mid-chukka or falls off, well, tough luck.

In fact, polo is a most difficult game to master, though you might not notice it from your side of a champagne glass. But when you stop a moment and think that the player is tearing down the field at 30mph, leaning precariously out of the 'sidedoor' of a 1,200lb pony while being tackled by the opposition, his left hand clutching the four reins of a bridle which controls a fast-moving, skidding beast while his right manoeuvres the 52-inch bamboo stick at the end of which is an inch-deep mallet head, it is not hard to see that this is a game where a successful juggling act is a feat of genius. Not only must the players be physically tough, but they must also be riding fit, their equitation standards second to none. As a game, polo is fast, dangerous and difficult, requiring high levels of skill and hand-eye co-ordination in addition to committed team work. However, none of this is much good without ponies of superior speed and handiness. Unsurprisingly therefore, the athletes to watch are the four-legged ones; what you might call pony power is often the most important winning factor and can amount to as much as 80 per cent of the battle.

Few matches are more fiercely contested than the International Polo at Smith's Lawn, for which the Coronation Cup and the Silver Jubilee Cup are the prizes. Two teams of four players challenge one another in matches divided into four, five or six chukkas, each one lasting seven and a half minutes. In the Royal Box is the Queen. The Prince of Wales is sometimes a player — in 1993 a team was put together for him by the Hurlingham Polo Association, polo's ruling body — the royal presence imparting a beguiling view of the monarchy as the Queen, in her role as a mother, drives herself to

watch her son polish his laurels at a sport at which he happens to be rather good.

The nearest spectators come to being part of the action is at half-time, when they are invited to step onto the field to tread in the divots of turf kicked up by the ponies' hooves. Treading the divots? This is peak socializing time and there is much more to half-time than kicking a few divots about the place. Half-time is the excuse to hobnob — frantically — before the bell heralds start of play once again. Already well tanked up with pre-polo drinks, this is the highlight of the match and a roaring success as acquaintances are renewed and invitations handed out. For some, this is what polo at Smith's Lawn is all about.

Polo has one other ingredient that gives it unique status on the Season's calendar. While first-time spectators may gaze in disbelief as players and their mounts swing up and down the pitch at great speed and under pressure in search of spurs awarded for sheer artistry of play, it so happens that what they are observing is a manifestation of 'serious leisure' of a type pursued only by the very rich. There are top dogs playing here, the kind who arrive by helicopter or Aston Martin; the offspring of industrial magnates and prestigious company chairmen, rich aristocrats and, of course, the Prince of Wales are amongst the few who can afford the prohibitive costs of high-goal polo. This is its strength, but also its weakness. While the excesses of sponsored sport are kept discreetly at bay — Cartier's sponsorship marquees are perhaps the exception rather than the rule — it is nonetheless a sport that a lack of money, spare time and manpower are putting under threat, according to the sporting press. Lloyds losses are to blame, so are Army cuts, they continue, and not a day goes by during the polo season without a whine about its 'inevitable demise'. No doubt we'll hear it all again in years to come, but while polo might wane, it will never die. Sponsors will continue to preside over it, and the Army, with its own teams, hasn't vanished entirely — yet.

The sport of the spectator is as vigorously pursued here as, say, at Royal Ascot down the road. The sartorial emphasis, however, is different: for the women, hats, for example, are not essential. At a sponsored event it is permissible to wear anything and most people do, though you would lose face irretrievably if you turned up in cut-off jeans and a

woolly hat. In the Guards Club's own enclosure, a tie is essential. Of course, the inevitable panama is much in evidence and some of the women do wear 'classic' little hats but, if anything, the idea is to 'dress down' rather than 'up' and you wouldn't necessarily dream of putting on for polo what is good for Royal Ascot. As film stars, polo wives and horsey females shimmy by, looking sleek and elegant if practical and understated, the message reads: too short, too tight, too big — far too Royal Ascot, in other words — has no place here.

Gossip, of course, is king of the spectator sports. Nobody really gives a hoot if the invitation to the Guards Club Enclosure 'got lost in the post'; it's the Cartier lunch marquee that counts. Some poor souls invited to neither are out braving the drizzle for the sake of the picnic. Rows of Rolls Royces and grander German cars suddenly find themselves supporting shanty towns of plastic beneath which lobster mousse, lemon-baked *poussin* and summer pudding are being eaten to the damp accompaniment of water trickling in rivulets down the neck and around the ears.

In the Cartier tent, rain doesn't even feature as invitees lunch together, eyeing up their companions, who might range from the illustrious to the downright inglorious. Here, TV newsreaders, blue-bloodied grandees, polo-oldies, fashion groupies and sexually ambiguous LA film stars search for something to chat about, all of them united for an hour or two in what comes easiest to most people, whatever their background: freeloading. Champagne, a three-course lunch, fine burgundies, shelter from the rain in dazzling company — these are what they're after and the polo players and the tempo of the sport are the luxuries that add lustre to the event.

After lunch, a bell rings signifying start of play. Only the hardened polo-oldies move to their feet and make for the grandstand. The rest, shamefully, carry on drinking and socializing because the Season *is* about being sociable. It is a mutual admiration society that gives the participating spectators a sense of satisfaction at their own social success. No relief is greater than that which erupts on the day the Cartier invitation to the polo at Windsor arrives. Only the refuseniks looking in through the gates — or, in this case, across from the other side of the polo field — know how bitter is the taste of exclusion.

INSIDER TIPS

ʊ It is not very chic to arrive too early for pre-polo drinks in the Cartier tent. On the other hand, remember two things: complications may arise in the journey to Smith's Lawn because the right gates are fairly difficult to find (make sure you know well in advance where to go); the later you leave, the less time there is for chit-chat before the first chukka.

ʊ If a number of you are going, a problem will arise: who will abstain from drinking? Make life simpler and find a chauffeur.

ʊ Trousers are fine for women on this occasion, stilettos are not. Women who wear them sink into the divots and end up looking ridiculous.

ʊ At the lunch, prepare to be gregarious; you may never have met your lunch companions and you may never see them after but, since Cartier has tried extremely hard to place their guests alongside interesting people, make an effort. Some don't.

ʊ Remember to keep well away from the field of play and from horses, pony lines and areas used for practice. Polo is a dangerous sport.

GLORIOUS GOODWOOD

JULY

THE GOODWOOD RACECOURSE in Sussex is in the tenth Duke of Richmond and Gordon's backyard. Along with Goodwood House, it's his, and so are those 12,000 acres on the southern slopes of the Sussex Downs surrounding his ancestral seat. Crowning the top of the Downs, this demesne looks out over undulating countryside far away to the coast at Chichester Harbour and the sea shimmering beyond: Glorious Goodwood they call it. There's no drama in this beauty. All hedgerows and fields, it's an idyllic, pastoral England of a type that colonials see in their mind's eye when homesick.

One distant view contains the point of the spire of Chichester Cathedral looming up at the end of an avenue like something in a Constable landscape painting. Further on, its counterpoint is the racecourse's Sussex Stand, which rises cathedral-like to dominate the approach from London. This award-winning piece of architecture confirms Goodwood's place in the twentieth century: 'The place to see . . . and be seen', said *The Times*, echoing the chronicler of Britain's built environment, Sir Nicholas Pevsner, according to whom it is the most beautiful racecourse in England.

Although King Charles II established the HQ of English racing on Newmarket Heath in Cambridgeshire, it was the descendants of the illegitimate offspring of his liaison with Louise de Querouaille, Duchess of Portsmouth, who created the racecourse at Goodwood. The third duke introduced racing onto a part of the Goodwood Estate known as The Harroway in 1801. So successful was it that he subsequently organized a three-day meeting under Jockey Club rules the following year. On the first day, he won with a horse called Cedar, but on the third day Cedar was beaten by Trumpator owned by the Prince of Wales, later King George IV.

Thus began an intermittent association with the Royal Family, culminating in the winning of the Sussex Stakes in 1909 by a horse belonging to Queen Victoria's son who, as Prince of Wales and later as King Edward VII, was a frequent Goodwood racegoer and house guest of the sixth duke. The Royal Family doesn't attend much any more, though five plaques in the Tapestry Room of Goodwood House record meetings of the Privy Council there — three of them held by Her Majesty the Queen. They took place at

Goodwood because race week normally coincided with the end of the parliamentary session. Only royal residences have hosted more such meetings.

The racing here is a key fixture for anyone devoted to the Turf, and has been since the fifth duke established Goodwood Races as a linchpin of the Victorian and Edwardian summer Seasons. Together with his friend Lord George Bentinck, he remade the race-course, the grandstand and, according to racing lore, British racing itself. In 1829 Bentinck and the duke sliced off the top of the Downs and brought in mountains of earth to create the final four-furlong run-in to the winning post. The impetus for this certainly wasn't commercial: it was the result of a genuine enthusiasm for the sport and the desire to ensure that ducal Goodwood hosted the best of racing.

What the present duke calls the drama of the Turf is still very much the attraction that brings Goodwood racegoers together. 29 July is Goodwood Cup day, the meeting's longest race (two miles), which was first run in 1812. While this is a tremendously important flat race, it hasn't always carried the prestige it does now. It used to be run in May and the move to July proved an immediate success and greatly enhanced the social status of the meeting. It coincided neatly with the end of the London Season and retained its relatively informal atmosphere, much appreciated by the aristocracy before they retired to their country estates for the remainder of the summer.

The Goodwood Cup is also one of the oldest races in the flat calendar and its roll call of winners is impressive. Priam, one of the best horses to have raced in the nineteenth century and an 1830 Derby winner, took the Cup in 1831 and 1832. Lester Piggott is its most successful postwar jockey. But the Sussex Stakes is arguably the most important all-aged race in Europe over one mile, and certainly it is the highlight of the Goodwood programme. Piggott is, again, its most successful postwar jockey.

To see his small, wiry figure galloping by is to witness in action one of the greatest jockeys of the century.

The racing at Goodwood is as good as any in the country, sometimes better, occasionally the best. It is at odds with the racing at Ascot in one important way: being far from London, it prevents international Ascot-only types from leaping into a car direct from Heathrow as they pursue the transatlantic social circus from one high visibility venue to the next. And yet, running for five days from 27 to 31 July, over 20,000 spectators still manage to get there on any one day.

Racegoers, on the whole, are a varied bunch. You see the extremes at Ascot and at the Derby, each one a caricature of their respective aspirations or backgrounds. The gen on horseflesh is not a prerequisite for attendance at either of those. Goodwood is a different story, however: here, the punters tend to know a thing or two about bloodstock, and because it is still a social event, an effort is made to look the part. The women might jam a hat on their heads — any old hat will do — but it is the men who tend to be the peacocks. While there is the usual smattering of battered panamas, well-used Racing Derbies and ancient or moss-coloured summer tweeds, others, like the Duke of Devonshire, take more pride in their appearance. 'Brown-and-white correspondent shoes are excusable at this meeting', he says, and he appears wearing a boater and a pale grey suit.

With nothing to prove, these Goodwood-ers are secure and confident in their mostly dowdy, shapeless summer wardrobes, expertly chosen for comfort and utility, particularly since the weather at Goodwood is anything but uniformly hot even if the racing is held at the height of the summer. These tough old hands cast looks of pity, even derision, at the fool who, following the dictates of fashion, came with bare shoulders, for they know she will depart before the end of the day, blue with cold. In fact there are times when Goodwood is far from glorious, though foul weather rarely ruins the day because the stoics of the Turf are oblivious to everything except horseflesh and jockeys and they are particularly fascinated by performance on rain-softened ground.

Glorious Goodwood will run and run, its peculiar attraction the beguiling cachet of an event run by an aristocrat. And even if that isn't your sort of thing, the excitement of top class horse racing brings its own rewards. After all, apart from 'July Week' there are thirteen other days of racing at Goodwood, spread throughout the summer.

INSIDER TIPS

★ A few sartorial hints: you cannot get into Goodwood's Richmond Enclosure without wearing a tie; take something warm, unless of course the day is assured of temperatures reaching 45°C in the shade. Nothing can be worse than a chill wind blowing at the Downs from the sea.

★ If, like the Queen Mother, you like a little flutter from time to time, take cash with you. The resident banks might not be your own and charges for cheques cashed are unavoidable. Most have no cash machine.

★ If your route from London takes in the A3 and the A286, take the turn-off from the former to the latter at Milford. If you continue on the A3 towards the alternative turning to the A286 at Hindhead, the stretch of road around the edge of the Devil's Punch Bowl, just prior to Hindhead, will slow you down.

★ Bring the usual racing equipment: umbrella, binoculars, hip flask and maybe even a small cushion.

★ Ditch Goodwood just a little before the end of the racing — if you want to avoid the traffic going back to London, that is.

COWES WEEK

JULY — AUGUST

THE COWES REGATTA is a world-class yachting event. Only the British could have invented it, given it a distinctly 'social' edge, then wedged it into Society's whirligig between Glorious Goodwood and the Glorious Twelfth. Eight days of yacht racing has long been seen as the natural next step after the racing at the Turf, and a key fixture to remember before the Society caravan rumbles on up North for the shooting and the stalking. Sportsman or not, if these things are important in your life, then there is little doubt that you wouldn't be seen dead anywhere else in the country but on the Isle of Wight, at Cowes, at the end of July and beginning of August.

The origins of this institution are rather hazy. Isle of Wight folklore traces it back to the races that were first organized for local fishing craft and the workboats of Cowes. Some say that its origins lie in the eighteenth century, when smugglers tried to outrun the Revenue's cutters. Certainly, there still exists a swashbuckling element. The date of the very first regatta, however, is not known for sure, though in 1815 a group of gentlemen formed the Royal Yacht Squadron and decided to hold a dinner and races every August. This event probably became a social occasion in the 1830s after Queen Victoria was drawn to Cowes for the summer by its quiet and relaxed atmosphere. The Queen's arrival as one of the earliest of the summer residents coincided with two trends which are thought to have fashioned the Cowes of today: the start of a vogue for seaside holidays which still continues, and the realization among young gentlemen that there was fun to be had from racing the fast sailing craft built on the island. Subsequently, the regatta became an international event.

Typically, the annual 'Week' is part-social, part-sporting, imparting a Jekyll and Hyde character to the ritual. The identity of the prevailing persona, and which of them is assuming control, is revealed only too clearly at times like, say, dusk, when the rounds of cocktail parties and dances begin in earnest, and that day's gruelling navigation of the Solent's famously capricious waters are completely forgotten.

Sailing and partying are the two key facets of the 'Week's' events: sailing is, admittedly, the more important, the races like the Fastnet being key sporting competitions for

international yachtsmen. Some Cowes-goers insist that while the 'Week' is an essential date in the Season, it is very much hands on, spectators off. Those who come for the partying might disagree, but then they may not necessarily know much about it, least of all how to distinguish port from starboard.

To participate fully on a grand scale — to be present when Society and the international yachting aristocracy meet — what you must have is permission to enter the Royal Yacht Squadron's hallowed premises in addition to an invitation to its Ball on the Monday. An invitation to the cocktail party on board the Royal Yacht *Britannia* would signal without question your social status, but if your invitations to both of these 'go astray', well, the fun crowd is to be found at The Prospect, home of Laura Aitken, Lord Beaverbrook's sister.

While the upper echelons of British Society and the grander international yachtsmen are doing it stylishly, the lower orders and the crews are confined mostly to a bunfight in the old West Cowes Marina, recently rechristened the Cowes Yacht Haven — not that its new name makes much difference to the ebullience of life led at the bottom of this parti-

cular social pyramid. In the mire, Cowes Week still has a lot to do with under-dressed blondes, beer swilling and being sick in dustbins. While Society is busily engaged in chitchat on the social whirligig, the hoipolloi and the penniless drunken crews are bungee-jumping or rocking the night away at Oracles, a disco housed in a shed. There are also possibilities for being entertained by live bands: in 1993 there was one called The Two Blue Nuns, which hung out in front of the Beer Marquee, a venue hailed by the local tourist board as 'the biggest bar in England'.

In between these two pinnacles of social achievement are the other clubs — the Royal London, the Island Sailing Club, the Royal Corinthian and the Cowes Corinthian. None of them is quite as stuffy as the prestigious Royal Yacht Squadron (which is to sailing what the Jockey Club is to racing), from whose balcony the races are directed and from whose start-line the sailing begins — at a signal fired from the club's own venerated cannon. This club is unquestionably the most élitist of them all, in spite of the fact that yachting is no longer really an élitist sport. 'The nobility and gentry are no longer coming to Cowes as they did once', somebody once moaned — and this was in the nineteenth century.

Even so, there are still 450 members of the RYS and they have to adhere to draconian dress codes: forget your reefer (a dark blue blazer) at your peril when on its sacred territory. Actually, all members have two reefers, one with black buttons for 'undress' and another with silver buttons for formal occasions. Very grand affairs require a mess jacket with black facings, dark blue waistcoat and trousers. God forbid that a member should turn up in a peaked skipper's cap, reefer or not. More railway porter than helmsman, this is the style of the parvenu who wants to be noticed and the RYS categorically is not for them.

The RYS sets the standards, and the other clubs trail along behind with varying degrees of egalitarian informality. At the Royal London, members and their guests have to wear a tie, while the Island Sailing Club requires simply that its members be 'smart but casual'. Down in the marina, anything goes: there is a significant influx of bandannas, rave hats and cut-off jeans. Deck hands wearing head scarves à la Bruce Weber render the old stalwarts of the Royal Yacht Squadron apoplectic with indignation. One thing never changes, though. Those who come just for the 'other' life at Cowes are the only people in pristine 'boat-wear' and matching separates from Simpson's, adorned with anchors and other nautical paraphernalia. A fo'c'sle is an alien concept and to them a poop is something dogs do. These are the people whose encounters with boats have been limited to a shuddering dally on board the Isle of Wight ferry.

Whatever your status, Cowes Week is good fun. And anyway, bandanna or reefer, upper crust or deck hand, when is a Briton happier than when he or she is watching the world go by over the rim of a glass? Not for nothing did one of the Sunday supplements in the summer of 1993 remark that the 'ten-day craziness begins again', bringing to the readers' notice the dawn of the 179th regatta and the apparent demise of reason and common sense amongst the serious yachting fraternity. 'Competitors plot a course towards an ultimate booze cruise', exclaimed another. Cowes Week's reputation is one of hedonistic display combining heavy drinking with tough sailing, a mix of alcoholic late nights and what has been called a 'gut-wrenching beat' up the island shore into a Force 6 the morning after. Exhausting but true.

In recent years, Cowes' unofficial figure head has been the Duke of Edinburgh, Admiral of the Royal Yacht Squadron. His patronage is the latest by a long line of sailing royals, of whom the most illustrious were Edward VII, Czar Nicholas II and the Kaiser, who was particularly struck by the event. Each morning, the Duke is ferried from *Britannia*, riding at her moorings off the RYS at the entrance to Cowes Harbour, to his boat, a public ritual which draws the crowds. Many people come simply to see the Royal Family at play and in 1993 they were able to watch the Princess Royal breaking with tradition by taking her own sailing boat, *Singlet*, to race and Prince Edward, as patron of the Ocean Youth Club, spending one day on its boat, the *John Laing*. Royal patronage inevitably raises the profile of an event, though Cowes, like Wimbledon, hardly needs it, so skilled are the yachtsmen involved. Sometimes the Duke, in spite of a history of royal yachting prangs, covers the Royal Family in glory: in 1993 he won the Landrover Trophy in his *Yeoman Twenty-Eight* with King Constantine of Greece at his side — the Duke's first win in thirty years — beating twenty-five other yachts.

There is no doubt that races in the Solent are tough — none more so than the Fastnet. Often it is very dangerous and winning a race — any race — is deserving of laurels. Catastrophes are not uncommon — your boat might wash up on a sandbank or end up grinding to a sickening halt on Grantham Rocks. Even royal yachts lack divine protection, as King Olaf of Norway found when his 40ft boat ran aground then sank in the first stage of the Admiral's Cup in 1993. But the daring and the speed are thrilling, never more than when hugely expensive yachts slither towards each other in seemingly unstoppable motion, an expensive collision avoided only by excellent judgement on the part of the helmsmen and crews.

The most extraordinary thing about the Cowes Regatta today, where it is significantly at odds with that rather great sporting event, Wimbledon, is its amateurish nature. Perhaps this is its charm, or perhaps it will spell its doom in years to come. But where else would you be able to race for the prestigious Admiral's Cup against the world's most experienced teams, and have, alongside, another race competing for the prize of a teapot?

INSIDER TIPS

⚓ Leave the Breton fisherman's jerseys at home, also the captain's caps. If you must put on 'boatwear' try Ralph Lauren's. Buy your blue Docksides at Pascall Atkey in Cowes High Street. They're the real thing. Binoculars are essential.

⚓ Book your car place on the ferry in advance.

⚓ The best view of the racing is from the Crab & Lobster pub in Bembridge or the foreshores at Bonchurch and Seaview. In Cowes itself, go to the waterfront promenade in front of the RYS — west of the castle — or Prince's Esplanade.

⚓ The place to eat is Murray's for the Isle of Wight's great seafood treats. Book well ahead: 0983 296233.

⚓ The Red Funnel ferries from Southampton to Cowes are less complicated than the Wightlink from Portsmouth to Fishbourne. The former crossing takes only an hour, the latter thirty-five minutes followed by a twenty-minute drive. See page 125 for details.

Tea at Betty's Cafe Tea Rooms, Harrogate

OPEN THROUGHOUT THE YEAR

ONE OF THE most famous places in England for taking afternoon tea was established in Harrogate in 1919: Betty's Café Tea Rooms. They flourish still, but who was Betty? After seventy years, her identity remains a closely guarded secret although, according to the tea rooms' menu, the stories about her are legion. None of them give any answers and Trudy the waitress, in her black-and-white uniform, wheeling a trolley on which wobble chocolate nut sundaes and strawberry meringue melbas, isn't telling.

Perhaps Betty never really existed. Whatever the truth of this mystery, nobody who's been to 'her' tea rooms gives the matter much thought anyway, in spite of the fact that 'her' name lives on. It has spread far and wide because of the excellent quality of the cakes and the tea and coffee sold there. In fact, a visit to Betty's is one of the key reasons for paying Harrogate, a handsome Yorkshire spa town, a summer visit. Betty's Tea Rooms are famed not just throughout the county, but further afield — connoisseurs from the capital and food reviewers from the national papers regard it as the closest thing to the perfect tea room.

As far as afternoon tea is concerned, the rest of the world takes its lead from the British. It's not a particular feature of the British Season, it's just a uniquely British daily ritual which takes place everywhere and anywhere. They do it at Henley, Ascot, Goodwood and Cowes, just as they do at The Royal Welsh Show and Blackpool, variations depending on the time of year, the company you keep and your specific location in Britain.

Summer's tea may be a picnic by the river, in which case it might include strawberries, clotted cream and a flask of stewing tea, or a flask of hot water accompanied by the teapot and the Fortnum & Mason's (or Betty's) canister of tea leaves. And, just as it's very civilized on a summer's afternoon to drink tea from china cups out in a field watching horses galloping by, or at a little folding table under the trees by the village cricket pitch, summer or winter you might also have it indoors — in the dining car on British Rail, or the first-class cabin on British Airways. At Harrogate, you have it at Betty's and at Bath, the Pump Room. The Glaswegians have it at the Willow Tea Room in Sauchiehall

Street and, if you're within a mile of Piccadilly, you do it at the Ritz or Brown's Hotel.

Afternoon tea — 'le five o'clock' the French sometimes call it — is also subject to local variation. At Betty's, it's more varied than most, a legacy of the establishment's founder, Frederick Belmont, who was a Swiss confectioner. Everyone knows that mid-European way with chocolate and pastry and what it does to the waistline. Nothing changes, and at Betty's this judicious meeting of Yorkshire Dale and Swiss Alp has been put to excellent use for the benefit of the burghers of Harrogate and tea's bewitching hour. Cakes, chocolates, bread, scones, muffins — over 400 different lines in all are still made by hand at Betty's bakery, bringing as much popular acclaim now as it did in the 1920s and the 1930s, when it basked in the glory of royal patronage. Special blends of tea and the best selection of coffees in the country come from Betty's own tea and coffee importing business, Taylors of Harrogate, and even Betty's wines are imported direct from family contacts in France.

Tea at the Ritz is dainty, and at Brown's Hotel you can only have it if first you submit to the dress code. A dress code? Since when does a collar and tie add to the enjoyment of tea and buns? At Betty's, the clientele have hollow legs and the ritual is a meal for which they roll in off the street, summer and winter. Daintiness doesn't come into it. It is one of the diet's key diary dates, for which anything can be worn — as is true of a typical

Viennese coffee house, which Betty's closely resembles. By 5.30p.m. tables are groaning with food and the queue at the top of the stairs is increasing, stretching to the door and out onto the pavement.

A cup of tea, delivered by a waitress in a black-and-white uniform, with toasted, spiced Yorkshire teacake, or cinnamon muffins or toast, or a warm Yorkshire fat rascal and butter, is unbeatable. But Traditional Afternoon Tea, according to Betty's menu, consists of roast ham or roast corn-fed chicken breast sandwiches, sultana scones with butter, whipped cream and strawberry jam, a Yorkshire curd tart and a pot of virtually any kind of tea you care to choose — from Special Estate Tippy Assam or Darjeeling, to China Rose Petal and Peppermint tisane, which comes served with honey. All for £7.33.

Alternatively, £3.66 brings with it just the sultana scones episode (with butter, whipped cream and strawberry jam) and the same list of teas. Calling itself the Cream Tea, this is anything but a minor meal and we haven't yet come to the High Tea section or the Evening & Brunch Specialities, the Children's Menu and the Patisserie, Desserts & Ices. Breakfast, brunch, lunch, tea, high tea, supper, from 9.00a.m. to 9.00p.m. seven days a week, Betty's will fill you up, allow you to read its newspapers or simply sit alone

and gaze out of the window or at the other clientele, who are an odd mixture of smoking and non-smoking old ladies in velvet tam-o'-shanters and smart young men-about-Yorkshire, their girlfriends, boy-friends or families in tow. In the evenings, a pianist at a white-painted upright piano serenades the patrons with 'The Way We Were' and 'Strangers in the Night', and they love it.

A visit to Chatsworth, or Harewood, or some other local country pile is best rounded off with tea at Betty's. It puts things in perspective, gives you a chance to digest the sights, discuss them and decide that perhaps, after all, you'd rather live somewhere more normal. Besides, walking about their gardens and down their long, cold halls is bracing — almost as invigorating as a walk on the Dales themselves — and therefore the best possible prelude to tea at Betty's.

INSIDER TIPS

🍵 Arrive a little earlier than you would normally for tea to avoid the crush.

🍵 Remember to take the papers with you, particularly if you go to Betty's for breakfast on Sunday.

🍵 Eat nothing before your visit. You'll regret it when you have to refuse the second hot-buttered pikelet.

🍵 Bring your Christmas list. Betty's has an excellent mail order catalogue and you can deal with all the friends and relations in one fell swoop.

🍵 If staying in Harrogate, and you have an arrangement to go to Betty's in the evening, leave the car at home and walk or take a taxi. Their wine list, if small, is excellent.

The Notting Hill Carnival

AUGUST

THE AUGUST BANK Holiday marks the end of summer — in theory anyway. How depressing. It reminds most of us, looking back over the past months, that the 'scorching' sun was never quite hot enough, that the thermometer, far from bursting, trembled only slightly, and the barbecue . . . it was hardly used and now it's rusting quietly away.

Everybody knows that the British weather can be notoriously unpredictable. And yet how bad can a summer be that has seen six test matches, the whole of Wimbledon, as well as the Notting Hill Carnival completed with hardly an interruption for rain, as was the case in 1993? Sunshine is essential to them all.

When it manages to push through the clouds, it inevitably heightens the exuberance of the Carnival in particular. This is a date out on the streets of London when, for two whole days, free-spirited mêlée envelops Notting Hill Gate. A procession of floats, dancers and loud, loud music thumps its gaudy way up Ladbroke Grove and along Westbourne Grove through London's W2 and W11 districts. Traffic is dispatched to other areas and the district succumbs to a seething mass of people of all races, colours and dress. Never quite as tropical as many of the Afro-Caribbean participants might want it to be, nonetheless the sunshine ensures that this event becomes the single most redeeming feature of a Bank Holiday Monday spent in London. Born out of racial strife in the late 1950s, this carnival, based on the Trindadian model, is now the biggest street party in Europe.

In New Orleans they call it Mardi Gras, in Salvador and Rio it is *Carnaval*. Each means a few days of mayhem as rich and poor partake in an orgy of music, dance and costume. Music hits you from every direction and you don't even have to understand it to enjoy it. As at Rio and other carnivals like it, the line between watcher and watched dissolves in a blur and at Notting Hill all spectators are potential participants. Everyone is encouraged to play and everyone has the right to join in, to jam the streets with sound systems, to dance behind the costume bands and to drink 'jungle juice' and rum and ginger beer along the route. Wear whatever you like, do as you please, there is a 'come play' attitude which is the essence of its success. And it isn't only Afro-Caribbean in content,

just in inspiration. In fact, the carnival is culturally all-encompassing and there is a bewildering array of offerings from the traditions of other sectors of London's hugely diverse population.

Loud sounds and violent colour and pattern are the distinguishing hallmarks of this particular event, which shake to their foundations the rotting terraced houses tottering down the Portobello Road, skirting Powys Square and running along Talbot Road. Windowpanes and dado rails pulsate in rhythm to the samba and the calypso, the soca sounds and hip-hop, the reggae and the ragga, soul, jazz, funk, zouk and revival emanating from the floats and the steel bands and the boogie boxes. Even the smug, stuccoed mansions graciously adorning the wider thoroughfares at the southern end of the district — up on the hill in Kensington Park Gardens, on Stanley Crescent and Ladbroke Square, even Holland Park itself — are blasted with an earful. The smells of burgers and onions, jumbo sausages and Smokey Joe's barbecued chicken legs and chargrilled corn on the cob waft into elegant drawing rooms and dingy basements alike, and for once the residents of Notting Hill Gate — as diverse a crowd as ever you could find in this famously heterogeneous capital city — are united for a few hours in the powerful evocation of Trinidad, Barbados or St Lucia.

The high point of the carnival is undoubtedly the procession of floats which are dragged, heaving and wobbling, along a designated route by lorries or, less glamorously, by tractors festooned with paper flowers and glittering swags of bunting made from shiny gauze and multicoloured cloth. Most resemble huge Christmas decorations, while others are like portable stage sets or junk yards, some of which are precariously constructed in two tiers so that each level is the territory of a different bit of the band.

Somewhere amongst all this, space is found for gorgeous, high-kicking female dancers who jive, shake their buttocks and grind their hips in time to the music, doing the congo, the porro or the guajira, oblivious of the dangers to which they are subjected as their teetering arenas groan and puff around corners from street to street. They urge the 'masqueraders' in front and behind the floats to greater and greater heights of dancing prowess, decked in a variety of costumes with themes as diverse as 'The Gathering of the Tribe' right through 'Visitors from Space' to 'Wings & Tings'. The chosen theme is interpreted through the dance, music and costumes, which are made from wire, cane, lamé, sequins, ribbons, feathers and fibreglass — the more ingenious the design the better. The ultimate aim of all this exotica is the hunt for a winner

As an important symbol of modern British urban culture, one usually maligned because of its other than trouble-free associations in the not too distant past, the Notting Hill Carnival fully deserves a place on the Season's calendar. It's as much an expression of British culture as, say, Ascot or the Royal Academy Summer Show because here you see the results of the influx from the Commonwealth enriching British poetry, slang, street life, cuisine and, above all, popular music. Nearly two million people flock to this tight grid of little squares and terraces to listen to the sounds of Notting Hill, thereby celebrating an important pathway on the road to racial tolerance. They can't all be wrong.

INSIDER TIPS

♫ At the risk of stating the obvious, leave handbags and bulging wallets at home. The crowds are thick and quick-moving — great camouflage for pickpockets.

♫ Go to Notting Hill by public transport. There is nowhere to park.

♫ Try to obtain a 'hand-out' locating different areas of the carnival, different bands, and so on. There are stalls along the route providing these and often the daily newspapers or listings magazines publish them as well.

♫ Avoid Ladbroke Grove tube station after dark. In the past, it has been the scene of indiscriminate muggings.

BUCKINGHAM PALACE

'WELCOME TO ONE'S home', shouted the *Observer* on Her Majesty's behalf, heralding her much-lauded plans for the Summer Opening of Buckingham Palace with an early preview of its contents. 'Buckingham Palace will be the biggest show in town . . .', it blethered on, echoing the London *Evening Standard*'s billing that this was the hottest tourist attraction in the capital in the summer of 1993.

Ever since the preceding April, when the Queen announced that she would open the palace to the public in order to raise funds for the restoration of Windsor Castle following the fire there, newspapers had been awash with speculation about what lay within. 'Inside Buckingham Palace' guides flooded the news stands, none of them absolutely sure what to expect. One salivating tabloid, providing much-needed fodder for the public's voracious appetite for news on the royals, had an eight-page guide to the 'world's greatest stately home' in addition to a through-the-keyhole account of what footmen and monarch gossip about when they meet on the stairs.

If the Windsor fire brought with it any benefit, it is this: twenty of the palace's 600 rooms are now open, and will remain so for the next five years throughout August and September. Anyone can go inside. Alas though, there will be no Queen to welcome you in — much to the fury of the papers. 'Palace cast stays away as peasants view the pageant', screamed *The Times* churlishly. Opening times coincide with the Queen's summer holidays at Balmoral and any other arrangement would confuse the smooth running of the palace's function as royal office. As head of state and national hostess, Queen, and family, live above the shop, you might say. What happens after the initial five years are up is anyone's guess though, who knows, if Her Majesty shuts it again, she might well have a revolution on her hands.

What will they see on the tour of the palace, these £8.00-a-head guests? Certainly not Prince Edward's shoes for polishing in a row outside his door, nor Her Majesty watching telly. What they will see is a dazzle of gilt, ormolu, marble, brocade, crystal and mirror in one of Britain's finest but least-known interiors.

Much of Buckingham Palace is the work of John Nash, who died in 1835. His work there has been much derided as a specimen of wicked, vulgar profusion. Since then, these interiors have remained largely unknown and seriously undervalued. How many of us have ever seen them illustrated? Nash was never given a chance to complete his decoration — he was sacked before it was finished — and much of it was subsequently replaced or painted over, some of it by Queen Victoria and Prince Albert. Much of the re-decoration is of the Edwardian period, which gives it that overall air of red, white and gold, but enough Nash remains to afford a comprehensive re-evaluation of his work — he was an architect of extraordinary ability.

A walk around the State Apartments will overwhelm even the sceptics. The interiors are not only richly decorated but are astonishingly sophisticated and inventive. Here you see all the decorative arts — sculpture, painting, plasterwork, marquetry, scagliola, metal work — brilliantly integrated, each one of them of the very highest standards of crafts-manship. Here is a novel and striking palace style, expressive of the panache of a country that was at the height of its military, commercial and cultural achievement. The artistic synthesis is a culmination of the taste of the Regency period; George IV, fat, extravagant and adulterous, first as Prince Regent then as King, had been experimenting with architectural decoration for forty years and here, finally, he had the resources to indulge his tastes. He had a superb eye for artistic quality and was a matchless collector. See him, King in coronation robes, in Thomas Lawrence's swaggering full-length portrait in the State Dining Room.

Summer visitors enter by a side door, but soon find themselves in Nash's quadrangle, which they cross to enter the State Apartments through Nash's Grand Entrance, in other words the front door. They don't have to creep in sideways as in many historic houses. Beyond, a route takes them up Nash's Grand Staircase, through his Guard Room containing John Gibson's statue of the twenty-eight-year-old Queen Victoria ('Albert is not quite satisfied with the likeness,' she wrote in her journal, 'though the figure is quite correct and gives the impression of youth'), the Green Drawing Room with its gold ceiling, the Throne Room with the red chairs of estate used by the Queen and the Duke of Edinburgh, and the Picture Gallery, home to dozens of masterpieces, including some by Rembrandt, Rubens, Hals, Claude and Van Dyck — the core of the magnificent Royal Collection. Beyond, the Silk Tapestry Room is followed by a sequence of State Reception Rooms — Nash's State Dining Room with its seven portraits of the Hanoverian dynasty, the Music Room used occasionally for Royal Family christenings (most recently Prince William's), and Nash's White Drawing Room (with its huge mirror which swings open at state functions to reveal the Royal Family, hidden in the Royal Closet). From the Minstrel's Stairs the route leads back to the Marble Hall and the Bow Room and finally out past the gardens and the gift shop (with its boxes of chocolate crowns) to the exit.

One imagines that the visitors, clutching their tickets as they dodge the traffic to cross the Mall on their way from ticket office to entrance, won't be like the mob that galloped into Carlton House in 1811 when the Prince Regent opened his doors for three days. So eager were they to see its magnificent interiors that one person's leg was broken in the crush, others fainted and many women had their dresses reduced to rags — some were seen wandering about the garden almost completely undressed. Twentieth-century visitors queue to buy tickets and are submitted to airport-style security screening. Thus, Her Majesty's flunkeys defy anyone to break the rules.

INSIDER TIPS

♚ Go to queue as early as possible on the day you choose for visiting the palace. Take with you a newspaper and/or a flask of coffee and be prepared for a long wait.

♚ Take an umbrella: queuing in the rain in the Mall is an unpleasant experience.

♚ Leave cameras behind. Photography is not permitted anywhere within Buckingham Palace or its grounds.

♚ Visitors and their belongings will be subject to a security check before entering. Leave large bags or luggage at home or in the hotel.

♚ It would be a wise idea to brief yourself fully on the history and contents of Buckingham Palace before entry. Because of the crowds, and uncertainty as to whether the palace will continue to open once the initial five years are up, it may not be so easy — or even possible — to return for a second look.

THE EDINBURGH INTERNATIONAL FESTIVAL

AUGUST — SEPTEMBER

INTELLECTUAL STIMULATION IS what festivals are for, and Edinburgh's International Festival is no exception. Appropriately, an old sobriquet calls the home of this hugely popular annual event the 'Athens of the North' because, after all, as headquarters of the Scottish nation and traditionally, along with Aberdeen, Britain's brainbox, it has been the supplier to the world of doctors, missionaries, and mechanical engineers, not to mention the inventors of the telephone and television.

While Scotland also does duty as the land of romance, all misty bogs and swirling pipes, Robbie Burns and tragic kilted heroes, it is — and has long been — a multicultural, multilingual society as well. Pluralism is richly rooted in its culture and there is a cultural proliferation which is a source of fertility and strength. Unsurprisingly, the Festival is sustained — and has been for the last forty-seven years — with great success. Year after year, it expands and diversifies more and more. And although the city's residents don't always show it, they have a sneaking pride in their city — especially when it accommodates the rest of the world for three weeks at the end of August and early in September.

As with any festival, you dip in and out of it, sorting out the trivia from the meaningful. But here the list of events is so formidable in its extent and range that any grading from the inane to the significant is meaningless unless you have a terrifically low boredom threshold. Even the most culturally illiterate will find something at this festival to inflame their senses. The Festival is not simply a gigantic international cultural beano celebrating the higher arts of opera, music and theatre, painting and sculpture. Quite apart from the fact that it has an element of Scottish nationalistic endeavour — see the Military Tattoo on Edinburgh Castle's Esplanade which, in 1993, commemorated the 900th anniversary of the death of Queen (later Saint) Margaret and had as its storyline the history of the Scottish crown — in amongst the galaxy of buskers working the space by the National Gallery, the Romanian clog dancers and the bungee-jumping on the Meadows, its Fringe end is the largest annual audition in the world. Here, as a performer, you can really make contacts and get your breaks.

Alongside the official Festival, Edinburgh's annual source of international glamour, the Fringe runs its jaunty course, providing British and world premières for 249 shows out of a total of 1,129. All the major papers put in an appearance on its behalf, so do the television companies, the agents and the producers, as well as the directors of festivals around the world, who arrive in droves looking for new talent. Silly to waste an opportunity: if you have any nous, in popular slang 'you go for it'. And if, as a result, you think that the Fringe is a giant job market, you would be correct — an impression reinforced by the recent advent of awards for productions of excellent quality. These offer successful productions a run at a coveted venue such as Edinburgh's Georgian Assembly Rooms, and a run in the West End. Little wonder, therefore, that the 1993 Fringe was the biggest in the history of the Festival.

In fact the Fringe dominates Edinburgh during this annual summer invasion of performers and arts *aficionados* and not even the presence at the Festival proper of the St Petersburg Philharmonic, or Antonio Gades dancing in *Blood Wedding*, or even the quartet of theatrical giants Peter Stein, Peter Sellars, Robert Lepage and Robert Wilson, can

detract (thrilling though their presence might be) from its burgeoning popularity, whichever side of the footlights you might happen to find yourself. Even the most reclusive of residents cannot avoid being touched by the Fringe in some small way, whether because members of some revue are sleeping on their living-room floor or simply because the nearby and normally dark, ancient and usually silent wynds and closes are decked out in gaudy colours and resonate with laughter, music and voices.

The Fringe venues are the source of hilariously creative inspiration: once, *2001 — A Space Odyssey* was performed in the back of a Hillman Imp and on another occasion one audience watched a production from beneath the stage, sticking their heads up through holes in the boards. Should you venture out to buy your *pesto* sauce at the local deli, or attempt to make a call from the payphone around the corner, well, a two-woman situation comedy or a German political cabaret with jelly might be in progress and you'll have to wait. The Fringe becomes wilder and more exuberant with every passing year and the more the programme hints at displays of flesh and sex, the more sought after the event, even though the City Fathers, famously prurient in this department, seek vociferously to protect the locals from anything as mind-damaging as total nudity. Perhaps they missed the freak show in 1993, in which Jim Rose and his creepy weirdos — in particular, one Lifto — who at their most gruesome hung heavy weights from pierced bodily appendages while naked, lay about on beds of razor blades and ate live worms and cockroaches. All in a tent on Carlton Hill, the Athens of the North's own Acropolis, whose Parthenon was only ever half built.

Having said all that, the Fringe is just one of the side attractions attendant on the Festival proper. There are others — the Film Festival, the Jazz Festival and the Book Festival. While the first is not as glitzy as other festivals in its category — there are more deals struck at Cannes, and Venice is more picturesque — there are few festivals of film assembled with such a passion for movies. Forget the latest Kenneth Branagh blockbuster or Sharon Stone's major new sleaze piece, which the Odeon will inevitably première; here you'll see Cannes award winners and new and enticing local productions set in places like the Western Isles or Glasgow. As the *Observer* remarked, 'This is the festival to browse through, pop into, experiment with, take a chance on.'

The entire Edinburgh Festival in its myriad mutations pulls in about as many spectators as the other 500 annual British arts festivals put together. Far from the squabbles about money which normally dominate the arts in this country, here it is a big party and a reminder that the arts can simply be tremendous fun. According to Tim de Lisle of the *Observer*, 'It's a lark, an ordeal, a drinkathon, a holiday, a lot of hard work, a talent contest, a love-in, a rite of passage, an endurance test.'

And in case none of this is of the remotest interest and you still feel yourself marooned in a cultural wilderness, there is always the city of Edinburgh itself to look at, its incredible architectural wealth spread out between the craggy tenements and dark vennels lining the Royal Mile in the Old Town and the expansive squares and elegant Georgian buildings in the New. There are art galleries and museums, most of them of national importance. And there are parks and gardens, restaurants and pubs, and shops to poke about in. Edinburgh is anything but culturally bereft — even after the Festival has packed up and departed.

INSIDER TIPS

★ Take a jumper and a brolly. Remember that Edinburgh is on the same latitude as much of Siberia. In other words, it never provides Festival-goers with a full three weeks of non-stop blazing sunshine. It is highly likely that adverse weather will inflict itself on you for at least some of the time, so come prepared.

★ Take a cushion. Many hours a day on hard wooden seats causes Festival Bottom, which isn't very comfortable.

★ Unsold tickets are available at the venues themselves from an hour before the performance. The Half-Price Ticket Booth in Princes Street Gardens sells half-price Festival tickets for that day's shows only, 1—5p.m. (a maximum of two tickets per person). Advance and daily bookings are also possible for the Film, Jazz and Book Festivals and for the Military Tattoo — see page 126 for details.

★ The people of Edinburgh don't live on chips and pints of Tartan bru'; here you'll find the best collection of restaurants in the UK outside London. You can eat well and at almost any price, choosing from a wide range of cuisines. Remember to book two or three days in advance if you want to be sure of a table.

CHATSWORTH, DERBYSHIRE

SUMMER IS THE time of year to visit the country house. Every British county has a handful of them in varying states of magnificence or decrepitude, and the annual visiting season — Easter to October — is keenly awaited by international tourists, country house buffs and eager National Trust members alike, all of them anxious to see for themselves the ensemble of great house, contents and grounds intact. If it still has a resident grandee, all the better. It adds the human touch and there is always the possibility of chancing on milady eating her beans on toast on great-great-great granny's sofa, if not actually dishing out the tickets at the door. Country house visiting has become a national pastime and no summer weekend is complete without at least a visit, no matter how brief, to one of the great stately homes.

At Easter the sound of ancient casement windows and sashes being flung open echoes up and down the land as the owners of castles, manor houses and country palaces rid their tottering piles of winter's fug. Heirlooms are polished, tapestries dusted down, and the dry rot, the damp and the woodworm routed in readiness for the first visitors of the season. The paying guest is an absolute necessity these days, particularly for a house like Chatsworth in Derbyshire which, with its 175 rooms, 359 doors, 397 windows and 1.3 acres of lead roof, costs about £1 million a year to run.

Chatsworth is one of the great country houses of England. A seat of the Cavendish family, it is lived in by the eleventh Duke and Duchess of Devonshire. It is the focus of a vast Derbyshire estate and a repository for an enormous collection of paintings, sculpture, books, furniture, ceramics, glass and textiles, all of it accumulated over the centuries by generations of Cavendish lords, often by judicious marriages to wealthy, brotherless heiresses. It is often said of Chatsworth that it is the 'Palace of the Peak'; certainly it is one of the grandest houses in the north of England and much of what you see there today is the result of the lavish spending of the 'Bachelor Duke' (1790—1858), whose bills for rebuilding, readorning, enlarging and extending ran to around £1 million — about £10 million in today's money.

As you approach the house from the public road, you cross over the River Derwent, which wends its way through the park below the building — a big square block whose 'style, proportions and decoration, both inside and out,' says the Duchess of Devonshire in *The House, A Portrait of Chatsworth*, 'and the shape of the garden reflect all that was best in the golden age of architecture and the embellishment of a great building and its immediate surroundings'. This must be one of the most magnificent sights in England — and it looks as if it simply grew out of the hillside. Behind the golden yellow stone house, transformed from Bess of Hardwick's mid-sixteenth century house between 1686 and 1707 by William Cavendish, the first Duke of Devonshire, a steep wooded hillside is crowned by the Elizabethan Hunting Tower. To the south, lie a large formal garden and the Emperor Fountain, the latter designed and built by Joseph Paxton to resemble a similar fountain the Bachelor Duke had seen in Russia and with which he wanted to impress Czar Nicholas, who promised to come to stay at Chatsworth. All around is the park which, in the eighteenth century, 'Capability' Brown turned into the lush, gentle landscape seen today. At Chatsworth, Arcadia can be found. 'Arcadia' — a place of rustic happiness and quiet repose relying on nature for its inspiration, but which is itself man-made — is an idea inextricably linked with the growth and culture of the country house, the development of its landscapes, gardens and garden buildings. It found its greatest expression in the eighteenth century, and here in Derbyshire is an important example of it. For the British with their passion for gardening — now a national pastime — what could be better than poking about in someone else's patch to see how they do it?

Every day of the summer, about 3,000 visitors pay homage to this ensemble. Dutifully, they surrender their entrance fee at the door on the north side, wander through the ducal portals and on down halls clad in tapestries and carvings, hung with portraits and landscapes, and cluttered with ancient marbles and portrait busts of long-dead dukes and their peers. There are stately panelled chambers containing magnificent inlay furniture, ceramics and glass; adorning them, painted ceilings, carved marble, magnificent

wrought-iron and beautiful carved woodwork combine to create interiors the sump-
tuousness of which was unsurpassed at the date they were created.

But the visitors are not really all that interested in the artistic and cultural worth of
the treasures contained at Chatsworth. Mostly, they've come to gawp at the scale of life
led here — there are twenty-one kitchens, twenty-four baths, fifty-three lavatories and
seventeen staircases — and to see how the other half live, not to pronounce judgement
based on envy but, by way of comparison, to thank God for their own lot and for the fact
that their bills, when they come in at the end of the month, are not nearly as big as they
must be here. If they actually knew that the present Duke had had to find millions to pay
death duties to the Treasury following the demise of his father, the tenth Duke, they
would be eternally grateful that their lot is simpler and easier to manage, and for the fact
that the gilded William Kent side tables in the State Dining Room, handsome and glittery
though they may be, would be far too big for their rooms anyway. Do they know that the
eleventh Duke, even after he had flogged 42,000 Derbyshire acres and disposed of a Rembrandt, a Rubens and a Van Dyck sketchbook, amongst other valuable works of art, took
seventeen years to pay his bill?

Of course, there are the country house buffs who come to tut over the shifting of a
formerly correct but now altered arrangement of chairs, or to gaze at rare Boulle cabinets
or stamped and gilded leather wall hangings. They peer behind statues and run their
fingers over mouldings, but in the majority are those who are determined to find out
what lies behind the velvet curtains, or to look through the keyholes of shut, locked
doors and to imagine Her Grace saying her prayers at the foot of the enormous state bed,
her feet blue with cold.

In actual fact, Her Grace is most probably out with the cows, or on a horse, or confined to quarters somewhere quite homely and out of sight — probably near the kitchen
and within easy reach of bathroom and heater, where warm temperatures offer welcome
respite from the arctic conditions, even in summer, in her husband's ancestral halls.
These visitors might be surprised to find that many of Chatsworth's rooms were never
lived in — in the sense that they were never used for writing letters in and mending

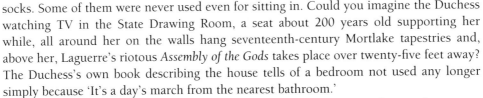

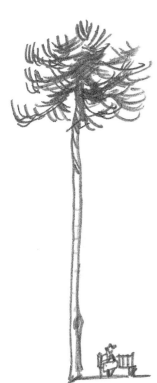

socks. Some of them were never used even for sitting in. Could you imagine the Duchess watching TV in the State Drawing Room, a seat about 200 years old supporting her while, all around her on the walls hang seventeenth-century Mortlake tapestries and, above her, Laguerre's riotous *Assembly of the Gods* takes place over twenty-five feet away? The Duchess's own book describing the house tells of a bedroom not used any longer simply because 'It's a day's march from the nearest bathroom.'

Coming to see how the other half live — and how they cope in this nearly servant-less age — is really the whole point about the stately home. It always has been. They were built for show, and even if rooms weren't ever used, at least hung with pictures and adorned with rich furnishings they could be admired and promenaded in. Ever since this house was built, strangers have been allowed to troop in to examine what was in the Devonshires' swagbag. And that the visitors might not pay much attention to the finer merits of one painting over another is really immaterial because often the builders of these princely piles themselves, in spite of having adorned them with Grinling Gibbons carvings, Van Dyck portraits of the wife and children, Laguerre ceiling paintings, or having asked Brown to improve on nature out in the park, did it only to assert their status. Often they, too, lacked any profound interest in the quality of the adornments. Here at Chatsworth there were exceptions from generation to generation, as the example of the present Duke shows — he has added works by Lucien Freud and Samuel Palmer, amongst others. But the aristocrat who threw his doors open to the public was a wise man, and he knew it. It kept the tumbrils out and stopped the public from demolishing the country palace out of envy or hatred. Both we, the public, and they, the owners of this stately heritage, continue in our traditional roles.

But come the last days of October and Chatsworth, like most other historic houses, prepares to boot out the last coach load of paying guests, lock the gates and pull down the blinds. For the past seven months or so, summer visitors have had a fascinating glimpse of life — then and now — on both sides of the green baize door, but now's the time to give the old fabric an overhaul in readiness for next year's visitors. They'll all be back, even if only for tea and a slice of the Duchess's walnut and almond cake in the stables' restaurant.

THE ARUNDEL ARTS FESTIVAL

AUGUST — SEPTEMBER

THERE IS SOMETHING terrifically beguiling about listening to music or watching a play in the open air. Sitting in the sunshine or reclining on a rug on a balmy moonlit evening, picnic hamper and drinks to hand, listening to or watching the events on a makeshift stage, has much to recommend it. If the backdrop, instead of being artificially constructed by set designers, is the wall of some old edifice, as it is at Arundel's Open Air Theatre, the mainstay of its annual summer Arts Festival, so much the better. Like Edinburgh's annual jamboree which has a brooding castle as its backdrop, Arundel has the ancestral home of the Earl Marshall and Chief Butler of England, the Duke of Norfolk, in its sights. Mostly mock-medieval, floodlit there cannot be many other venues like it, and there is little doubt that this is the place, if you just happen to be in Arundel over festival week (which begins near the end of August), to spend a summer evening.

Open air theatre is nothing new. The ancient Greeks were masters at it, and the locations they chose in which to set it were often sublime: imagine their theatre at Taormina in Sicily where, looking towards the stage from the seating in the auditorium, you saw not painted cardboard but a distant smoking Etna, the permanent backdrop no matter what was being performed. At Nora in Sardinia, the Romans constructed a theatre with a view to the ocean. At night there can have been few scenes more magical.

Then, in the hot Sicilian or Sardinian summers, the less you wore, the more comfortable you were. In the English summer the opposite is true; generally you throw on whatever keeps you warmest most comfortably, since summertime in Britain is no guarantee of good weather. The Arundel Arts Festival finds itself marooned in the south of England so is of the latter species, but practical considerations, such as those which involve body temperatures and comfort, give it an air of informality which has become its hallmark. Besides the Open Air Theatre, events are also staged in churches and there is a whole 'arts gallery trail' that threads its way in and out of the porches, hallways, kitchens and gardens of other people's homes, which are turned into temporary art galleries specially for the event. Here you are as likely to trip over the family cat as you are to discover the discerning critic doing an undercover rekkie of the displays. Those properties

doing the honours with displays of contemporary art — ceramics, watercolours, jewellery, sculpture — are marked with a striped banner hanging at their door.

The Arundel Festival came into being in 1977 when the Duke of Norfolk allowed Shakespeare's *Henry v* to be performed in the grounds of Arundel Castle. It was a great success and today the festival is one of the largest in the south of England. Every year the whole of the town blossoms, as for ten days the arts bandwagon rolls into town. In 1993, you could have heard Anthony Hopkins talking about Tchaikovsky in Arundel Parish Church. It was the composer's centenary and, also in his honour, the Primavera Chamber Orchestra delivered his Serenade for Strings at the same venue.

'The Seaside Deckchair Show' was one of the more inimitable happenings. It consisted of a show of deckchairs painted by artists and designers in a variety of stripes, splodges and squiggles, and was held within the unlikely confines of Arundel Castle itself. There, against the curtain wall, it was displayed, a splash of seaside England located incongruously in a historic fortress, to be sat on, tried and tested by no less than the Friends and Patrons of the festival, who were invited by the Countess of Arundel, President of their Society and daughter-in-law of the Duke, to investigate the results at a garden party on the Saturday at 3.00p.m. 'Do come and bring your friends to enjoy a real English tea', said the Arundel Festival Newsletter.

In 1993, too, the Open Air Theatre hosted a performance by the Oxford Stage Company of Shakespeare's *Comedy of Errors*. This alfresco venue was just one stop-off on a route that had taken the company from Farnham via Gdansk to this Sussex location. It was staged after Bank Holiday Weekend had been and gone, taking with it all the action and clamour attendant on the exploding fireworks detonated in time to Ravel's Bolero in the Firework Concert provided by the Band of the Grenadier Guards. This was a weekend of entertainment for the family: a mucky glory of sandwiches and crisps, orange juice and chocolate wolfed down at the Medicine Show — where rope-walking was combined with melodrama and stage combat — accompanied by the Rhythm Doctors, 'fine musicians bringing a strong streak of comic fantasy to their jazz'. There was Humphrey Lyttelton and his Band, and the London Mozart Players, who gave a 'blend of tonal

balance and stylistic accuracy' (*CD Review*) in the august surroundings of the Baron's Hall deep within Arundel Castle. In honour of all this, formal seating was dispensed with throughout the weekend. All you had to do was remember to bring your own picnic and a bottle opener.

Such festivals will have all the allure of a mythic Englishness as long as they also have the right components — big house, parish church, village shop, high street, and so on. Although a small town rather than a village, Arundel in Sussex incontrovertibly conveys the essence of this myth. Straddling the River Arun, rising on the slopes of the South Downs, it is dominated by the historic Church of St Nicholas, the Catholic Cathedral, and an aristocratic stronghold, part-medieval part-nineteenth century, which has formidable associations with centuries of English history and which must be one of the noblest sights in England. All around the town, the Norfolks' acres protect this settlement from overt expansion; fields and pastures run up to the gardens of the medieval, Georgian and Victorian houses, and there are meadows, woods and tree-filled glades fulfilling the idyll of a rural England at its best. On the river, swans, in the high street, teashops and pubs, and little mellow houses tumbling down to the Arun at the bottom of the hill. Everywhere, heraldic references — medieval or mock-medieval — carved in stone or wood, allude to the heritage of Arundel's illustrious masters — a great many of them capricious lords who spent more time in than out of the Tower of London.

While other festival venues cannot match all of this, it is true to say that the Arundel Festival is not exactly in the same league as October's heavyweight literary festival at

Cheltenham, nor is it as big, or as internationally popular, as the nearby Chichester Festival of Theatre with its troupes of famous actors and actresses. It may not carry the weight of Glyndebourne, to which opera *aficionados* stagger under the weight of picnic chairs, hampers and champagne, in black tie and evening dresses, but of them all there is so much on the periphery to recommend it that this arts festival, on balance, is a better all-encompassing English summer event.

Apart from its scale and the fact that most of those attending are country people living locally, there is its relative rusticity, defined by the tone of its events and the venues in which they are set. Its popularity derives, at least in part, from its location and its indications that country life is alive and kicking. As if to prove this point, the Arundel Festival has also taken to staging events in outposts in its orbit — Littlehampton, Amberley, Boxgrove and Clymping.

An arts festival located in relative rusticity is most appropriate. Only until relatively recently were the arts and letters anchored firmly in country life, and music, too, has its origins in the songs and dances of rural seasonal festivals. It comes as no surprise to discover that Hesiod's *Work and Days*, the first great Greek text after Homer, was a kind of agricultural manual and more recently, by comparison, the paintings of Constable, the poetry of Wordsworth and the novels of Thomas Hardy, for example, are firmly rooted in a celebration of the ultimate truth which lay in an agrarian setting rather than an urban one. Even the annual exhibitions at the Royal Academy were dominated by country scenes until well into the twentieth century. Sir John Betjeman was the last major poet to revere rural England and now rustic images are fading fast from our culture as we seem to lose touch with the dignity of country life. That we need it was articulated by John Major, when he invited us to share his vision of an England of warm beer and cricket.

Perhaps a necessary step in the realigning of these threads with our history is the foundation of the arts festival in rural locations such as this one. Festivals of all descriptions are blossoming — and flourishing — all over the rural heart of England, just as surely as what have been called the 'shires novels' of Joanna Trollope and Mary Wesley, which, like Radio 4's 'The Archers', are becoming a cult. All of this is certain to continue.

INSIDER TIPS

★ Make a phone booking; the box office opens in July. All major credit cards are accepted for orders over £10, or they hold bookings for forty-eight hours to give a cheque time to arrive in the post.

★ Book in person; a trip to Arundel is worth the effort, any summer's day.

★ The festival's restaurant is in the Tea Lawns in the Castle. Make a reservation for dinner at least twenty-four hours in advance.

★ Take something warm for an alfresco performance in the Open Air Theatre — warm clothes, rugs, anything.

★ Since many of the venues take place in a range of churches with hard wooden pews, take a cushion.

ALTON TOWERS

MARCH — NOVEMBER

MAROONED IN A bucolic corner of the Staffordshire landscape that typifies the rural idyll of England in the summer, is Alton Towers, the theme park 'where wonders never cease'. It's the kind of place to which the *Sun* newspaper, mindful of its revenue, entices its readers with lurid pictures of screaming kids being rocketed into space on some contraption guaranteed to induce maximum thrills through speed and the notion of impending peril. 'A scream come true', yelps the *Sun*, a four-page 'fun offer' giving added scope to a contentious issue: how to amuse the family on a boring summer weekend. 'Euro hols? We'd rather go to Alton.'

The biggest wonder of all makes itself known to you as you wend your way towards this 'great day out' through winding lanes, past villages hidden in little valleys, and woods and hedgerows. Alton Towers really isn't the blight on the landscape that you had imagined it to be having read about it in the *Sun*. This is very surprising; Europe's most successful theme park, where over 60,000 burgers, 415,000 pounds of chips and 390,000 hot dogs are consumed in the average season, is actually rather well hidden. It is screened by 200 acres of woodlands and a densely planted garden filled to bursting with ornamental architecture, most of it put there in the nineteenth century by the fifteenth Earl of Shrewsbury, whose monstrous Victorian Gothic family seat, Alton Towers, was abandoned by his descendants in 1924.

Nonetheless, the existence of Britain's No. 1 theme park in the fifteenth Earl's gardens causes a *frisson* of disapproval to ruffle the feathers of the garden history buffs, who swoon within the orbit of an original surviving landscape. Yet their whining is misplaced. Perversely, the sense of pleasure that today's theme park, with its stomach-churning Corkscrew and Black Hole Roller Coasters, Waveswingers and Katanga Canyon Rapids Ride, incites in the punters is in a similar vein to what Lord Shrewsbury intended when he filled his ancestral gardens with ornaments and conceits. His rocky dell, the blind retainer he housed in the Harper's Cottage (whose role was to play the harp, thereby contributing to the emotions of those wandering by), the conservatory whose design evokes the Arabian Nights, the Chinese pagoda fountain, and the small, abridged version

of Stonehenge, are a classic Arcadia gone mad. It was a feast on the eye, an amusement and then, as now, there were thrills to be had by all.

Besides, in answer to the wails from those buffs who always want everything back as it was — in this case, nothing less than the complete removal of the white-knuckle rides, the burger bars, the flashing lights and piped music from its little patch of Staffordshire — in 1860 the eighteenth Lord Shrewsbury himself used the place as a showground. Having staged a magnificent triumphal procession to mark his inheritance of the estate after a battle with the Duke of Norfolk, to whom it had been willed by the seventeenth Earl, he went on to open the grounds to the public so that, by 1890, Alton Towers was attracting crowds of 30,000, who came to view acrobats, lion tamers, performing elephants, bands, fireworks displays, as well as the by-now mature gardens. The gardens were open every day in the summer and special trains were laid on from the Midlands to cope with the crowds curious to see such unlikely things as the woman who lifted a live horse, caught a cannon ball fired from a cannon, and had a cannon fired from her shoulders. Far from turning in his grave at the tramp of those 2.5 million modern feet visiting Alton Towers each year, one imagines that Lord Shrewsbury, were it possible, would be out there holding open the doors of the monorail, welcoming the punters in, if not selling them tickets and directing the traffic. After all, it's what many stately home owners do these days anyway. The People are winning and not a tumbril in sight.

At Alton Towers you hear grown men squeal like babies. Pleasure? Torment? Put them on the Corkscrew Roller Coaster or the New Beast, fasten their safety belts and let them have it. Slowly, an ornamental bullet into which you're strapped climbs gently and gradually from the station, up a sort of railway line, to a great height from which there are marvellous views out over the countryside. Everyone is lulled into a false sense of security. Then, suddenly and without warning, you are rocketed downwards, the great speed impaling you against the seatback. Your cheeks scramble unflatteringly, and your hair and clothes stream behind you as if in reincarnation of the last episode in the life of Isadora Duncan. If you're not careful, you might see your breakfast again that day, shooting by in the opposite direction as the descent twists and turns, loops over and under, gathers speed then hurtles you on up for more. Grown men do indeed squeal, as do their wives — this is inevitable when they're rocketing down a 60ft drop at 50mph with a deceleration producing pressure of 4G.

In the Black Hole you spiral upwards before a terrifying 50ft drop and, while you're reaching 45mph with a force 2.5 times greater than gravity, you're in the dark — literally. The Black Hole is the original nightmare. This appalling experience, for which people return time and again — 'we'll be back', says trucker dad Joe and wife Val — is mirrored by the Haunted House experience to which the under-twelves love to subject themselves. 'Ooh, Mum, a ghostie.' A ghoulish freak jumps out of a corner, its mad red eyes rolling horribly while it vomits smoke and bloodcurdling screams which envelop the little ghost train that rattles its way around the tomb-like hind quarters of the haunted house. 'Ooh, Mum, it's better'n the last time.' Wide-eyed with horror, the kids love it.

But perhaps best of all are the Congo River Rapids, for which everyone sheds all remaining dignity. Huge rubber tyre-like 'rafts', on which are perched little seats, bounce along a half-mile canal — they call it the Katanga Canyon — through which five and a half million gallons of water swirl every hour, with another 20,000 gallons cascading down the waterfalls into it every minute. You clamber onto the rafts and away you go, bouncing about, swirling in the turbulence and praying that you don't get a dunking.

Madness and reckless abandon prevail everywhere you look. Even the ruined mansion is only really a folly now that its interior has been demolished. Long abandoned by its aristocratic earls after 700 years of ownership, its empty hulk is a shadow of its former self and from its hillside it broods over the crazy scenes of Margate's annual summer meeting with Blackpool down below. The Alton Towers experience is very much a part of the modern British Season simply because it is so classless. Out there on the rides, guzzling burgers and chips, or shrieking with the crowd, there are those who, albeit surreptitiously, are happy to exchange the exclusivity of the traditional Season, simply to avoid being buried alive in the traditions of old England, for this new version of it. Nothing could be further from that stronghold that shows England to be a monarchical country with an aristocracy — Royal Ascot — and nothing could be more popular.

INSIDER TIPS

Get there as early as you can. It fills up really quickly, which means the queues for the rides are longer.

Breakfast lightly — remember, those rides tip you upside down.

Ask about special tickets for a two-day Alton experience, or for reductions if you take the whole family.

Picnics are not really necessary — Alton Towers has a huge variety of eateries from which to choose a meal.

THE ILLUMINATIONS, BLACKPOOL

SEPTEMBER — NOVEMBER

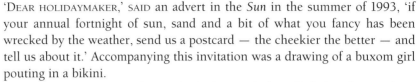

'DEAR HOLIDAYMAKER,' SAID an advert in the *Sun* in the summer of 1993, 'if your annual fortnight of sun, sand and a bit of what you fancy has been wrecked by the weather, send us a postcard — the cheekier the better — and tell us about it.' Accompanying this invitation was a drawing of a buxom girl pouting in a bikini.

The *Sun* cut right to the quick of what might be called 'the Blackpool experience': sea, sand and sun, and sex. If the weather prevents visitors from fulfilling their needs in any one of these departments, they have a choice: they could either simply catch a plane exceedingly quickly to one of the Spanish coastal resorts, or they could do as the *Sun* suggests. Or, they could sally forth to Blackpool's Golden Mile, there, under the dazzling glare of its Illuminations, to spend their holiday pay in the amusement arcades, the slot machines, the restaurants, theatres, cinemas, discos or the blue, late-night adults-only shows.

A fortnight is about the average length of the British working man's holiday break. And how better to spend it than by taking a trip in the fresh air to the seaside, to which as much ritual attaches as, say, an outing to Ascot or Cowes. This is Britain's annual seaside pilgrimage, its space in summertime's calendar allotted to it as a result of the Victorian craze for sea air, sunbathing and swimming. The seaside ritual nowadays, apart from providing opportunities for dunking yourself in the freezing Irish Sea, is about fishing from one of the town's three piers, paddling at the water's edge and donkey-riding across the sands — provided you're under sixteen, under eight stone and don't kick, whip or use a stick against the beast, say the Regulations with Reference to Asses on the Foreshore. It involves eating ice-creams and getting plastered or laid, or both. Summer's seaside break signals prime leisure time in Britain, and amongst its most familiar vignettes are the Yorkshiremen and the Scotsmen on the promenade, who lie slumped in deckchairs sleeping deeply, knotted hankies on their heads, and the clutches of Bet Lynch (of 'Coronation Street') lookalikes — all peroxide bouffant and teeny outfit — down at the Empress Ballroom of an evening, cackling, cruising and drinking Dubonnet and Coke.

Picnicking is another essential ingredient of the seaside holiday experience — as indeed it is at Ascot or any other event taking place in the British summertime. Alfresco dining — lolling about in a deckchair on the promenade, leaning over the railings of a pier, or splayed out on the sand — is the supreme treat brought to Britons under cover of sunshine and nothing, least of all damp, gloomy weather, deters British picnickers from enjoying what has become theirs by right — and tradition.

At Blackpool no midday 'dinner' outdoors is better than delicious paper-wrapped fried fish and chips, topped with lashings of salt n'sauce, washed down with beer or a Fanta, and rounded off with a hearty belch. Unlike Ascot or Cowes or Wimbledon, where food is 'refeened' to a degree and, even outdoors, is consumed with knives and forks, at Blackpool the fish and chip lunch is a pig-out and its passage from paper to mouth is assisted by naked fingers. If this is preceded in the early hours of the day with a robust helping of eggs, bacon, sausage and chips, so much the better. In fact, by 9.00a.m. on a typical Blackpool summer Sunday, some half a million eggs have been cracked and served up with two million rashers of bacon. By midnight, it is reckoned that two large herds of pigs will need to have been slaughtered to feed the bacon, sausage and pork-pie habit of the visitors, not to mention the forty acres of potatoes that will have been dug up in order that this indulgence might be accompanied by great piles of chips.

Blackpool is a hugely popular venue of the British holiday season. It has gone from strength to strength ever since the first visitors were drawn to sample the healthy attributes of its coastal waters in the 1720s. One William Hutton, visiting in 1788, wrote that

'The inferior class['s] . . . sole motive for visiting this airy region, is health . . . The rich rode in carriages or on horseback along the sands, while poorer visitors find equal pleasure in using their feet.' Nowadays, a visit still allows you to brave the freezing Irish Sea though, unlike earlier visitors who liked to drink the sea water thinking that its beneficial properties were better imbibed by drinking it than by swimming in it, caution is advised, since Britain's coastal waters are not what they were.

The arrival of the railway in 1846 brought in its wake an entertainment boom the tremendous success of which led to the blossoming of a seaside circus complete with opera house, Winter Gardens, the famous Blackpool Tower and a whole host of theatres, all of it provision for indoor entertainment. Luckily there is — and was — a lot of it because inevitably, being Britain, Blackpool and other seaside resorts like Bournemouth, Weston-Super-Mare, Whitley Bay, Llandudno and Minehead are subject to appalling summer weather, deluges forming a large part of this.

But Blackpool, of them all, has a distinct advantage over the others because, in addition to its Golden Mile of stage shows and dancing venues, it has the Illuminations, of which it is justly proud.

These are 'The Lights', and they are an after-Season event. 'Simply Brilliant', scream the brochures. 'It's nicer with the lights on!' People flock to this Lancashire town to see them and whatever beauty Blackpool can muster is borrowed from the darkness of night — and man-made light. With their help, Blackpool claims to attract more visitors than Greece and the Greek Islands, and has 120,000 holiday beds — more than the whole of Portugal. When local officials

switched on the very first display of lights on Princess Parade in 1912 — to mark the visit of Princess Louise (the first ever visit by a member of the Royal Family) — one of Britain's most remarkable and enduring tourist attractions was born. Nowadays, Blackpool's tourist season goes on well into November, prolonged by The Lights, which are switched on early in September — just as the season is winding down around Britain's coastline. And when the last pretence of summer has long been abandoned everywhere else, here the hotel prices go up, not down.

Victorian Blackpool was the first town in the country to 'go electric'. A century later, the resort's flirtation with light endures — though much refined with fibre optics and computer controls. And the Illuminations are the focus of special coach trips to Blackpool — which seems odd when you think that admiring electricity is a remarkably old-fashioned thing to do. Stretching along the seafront for over five miles, they transform the promenade into an enormous funfair. The 'switch-on' is now the high point of Blackpool's summer diary and is bestowed with a status akin to that of *Britannia*'s arrival at Cowes, or the Queen's drive onto the Turf at Ascot. A celebrity is always invited to 'do the honours' by flicking that switch: in 1949 it was Anna Neagle, and in 1958 Jayne Mansfield very nearly eclipsed even The Lights, accomplishing what history likes to call the 'turn-on' of the Blackpool Illuminations. Danny La Rue, Tony Blackburn, the entire cast of 'Dad's Army' and 'Coronation Street', and Kermit the Frog have all taken their turn. Even the horse Red Rum, in 1977, was led between two winning posts to trip the inaugural switch.

Blackpool after dusk is an adventure. The great tunnels of light, the tableaux and illuminated displays like, say, 'Canine Capers' (in which a selection of pet dogs are got up in humorous poses) and 'Time Marches On' (in which animated clocks wink at the visitors) and other obscure delights, are a gloriously tacky and absolutely free novelty well worth making the effort to see. After all, the sixteen and a half million annual visits made to Blackpool cannot all be made in vain. Quite simply, there is little doubt that Blackpool, much scorned, is one of Britain's unsung delights.

The Royal Highland Games, Braemar

DURING THE FIRST few days of every August there is a feverish eruption of activity amongst the Old Guard British. It is the signal that the time has come to quit England and head north for the Highlands, where the Scottish Season is about to begin.

The patron saint of its outward-bound hunting, fishing and shooting participants, St Slaughter, is goaded into action; the 'Glorious Twelfth' marks the kick-off. This August day sees the first guns out on the grouse moor bagging birds which, if shot in Scotland, are then flown to London in great haste so that they can be served to diners that very night — at staggering expense. And there is the salmon river to be fished and the deer in the hills to be stalked. These are social 'games', each with a set of rules to be followed, each requiring vast expenditure of physical energy. And then, providing the social rallying points between kills, there are the house parties, the balls and the Highland Games, of which the Gathering at Braemar, held on the first Saturday in September, is possibly the best known.

Up North, fusty shooting lodges are opened up and aired in readiness for the mêlée. Guns are cleaned, fires lit — even in the summer — and bottles of whisky are heaped into drinks cupboards up and down the hills. The Scottish Season is an exhausting and thirsty business and the hostess who has gallons of whisky at the ready is a wise planner. By now, those whose summers are always spent north of the border have bagged their berths on the sleeper from King's Cross Station to Inverness. Such preparations are made months in advance. Even the venerable hand-me-down kilts are long since back from the demothing establishments, neatly pressed and ready for action at the Lochaber Ball, or the Northern Meeting, or the balls at Oban or on Skye. But the practice runs for those who've forgotten the intricate steps of 'The Reel of the 51st' or 'The Dashing White Sergeant' are still in progress and will remain so until the hour to depart for the balls has arrived. Absolutely nothing matches the fury of those in the reeling fraternity who find themselves partnered with an ignoramus from London who doesn't know how to reel. Nothing is worse than a Sassenach who cannot keep up.

The Royal Family — or at least some of it — heads the exodus, its annual pilgrimage

P.114

taking it to Balmoral Castle, Victoria and Albert's stately pile on the banks of the River Dee not far from Aberdeen. Of the surroundings, Victoria wrote in 1852: 'The view is more magnificent than can be described, so large and yet so near everything seemed, and such seas of mountains with blue lights, and the colour so wonderfully beautiful.' Inspired, no doubt, by their ancestor's praise, there the Royals remain for the whole of August and September, emerging only if an occasion absolutely requires their presence.

The Braemar Gathering is one of these: by attending in person, the Queen is carrying on a tradition set by Queen Victoria who, in 1848, presiding over the games for the first time in her reign, was symbolically taking the place of King Malcolm Canmore whose father, King Duncan, was murdered by Macbeth in 1040. A legend has Malcolm, who had a hunting lodge at Kindrochit, Braemar, summoning the clans to the Braes o' Mar in order to select the fastest runners and the mightiest muscles for his bodyguard. Victoria, smitten by the romance of all of this, became patron of the games and, ever since, the reigning monarch has made a visit to the Royal Highland Gathering a fixture of the annual Scottish retreat.

Highland Games are a highly entertaining aspect of the Scottish summer. Someone once described them as 'a cross between a nationalist rally, an international village sports meeting and a trouserless eisteddfod'. But they are really 'an exhibition of Highland sports in which physical strength and dexterity are combined', as a contemporary account put it 118 years ago, talking about Braemar in particular. There is an air of carnival, and there is colour, excitement and tension as local teams of 'heavies' — shot putters, caber tossers and hammer throwers — clad in vests and kilts, prepare to pit their strength against one another for a winner's trophy. On a sunny day in early September the Braemar Gathering, which takes place in The Princess Royal and Duke of Fife Memorial Park situated in a natural arena in the heather-clad hills of Royal Deeside, is also a beautiful place in which to while away a few hours. This and the ever-present attendant skirl of pipes accompanying dancers doing the Highland fling (the sword dances are thought to derive from the time when Malcolm Canmore placed his sword over that of his vanquished foe and proceeded to perform a dance of victory over them),

is a sight and a sound that symbolizes the games to the Scot both at home and abroad.

But the games at Braemar are not unique. In fact, a smarter sort of Scot tends to avoid this paparazzi-ridden occasion and instead goes to the Blairgowrie Gathering at Ardblair Castle. In addition, a great many Scottish villages have their own games, in which teams compete for prizes in those competitions already mentioned — and others besides: tug-o'-war, running races, wrestling and Highland dancing. Any games has these events and is run along traditional lines, but each is subject to local variations from which it derives its own identity.

The Strathardle Highland Gathering in the Perthshire village of Kirkmichael, for example, has a variation on musical chairs — using cars. The participants also play something called Tilt the Bucket, and The Greasy Pole. In the latter, two pillow-fighters compete to unseat each other from a smooth and shiny horizontal pole supported above the ground by two vertical posts. And here, according to Helen Nicholson, a local resident who never misses a single gathering if she can possibly help it, 'The beer tent is a haven.' The beer swillers slosh about as if there was to be no tomorrow, then totter off to the ceilidh in the village hall, where Jimmy Fairweather and his Band have been engaged

to accompany the whooping, sweating hooley until the 'wee small hours', when it falls down in exhaustion. By contrast, at Braemar a drink is hard to come by and, when found, its consumption is very strictly controlled.

The local laird or his representative is invariably present: at the Braemar Gathering the arrival of the royal party in a series of enormous black limousines is presided over by the Lord Lieutenant of Aberdeenshire, currently the Chief of the Clan Farquhar, who, re-splendent in his family tartan and magnificent emerald-green tweed jacket, welcomes the Queen to a peculiar wooden bothy adorned with branches and bunting — a structure not unlike a garden shed dressed as if for a harvest festival. Assorted local grandees — like the Duke of Fife, who is descended from King Edward VII's daughter Princess Maud — pay homage; so do the 'people', the latter with their little bunches of white heather, which are presented to the Queen and the Queen Mother. Monarch, duke and clan chief are all fulfilling an almost feudal role as lords over thousands of acres of surrounding territory. They present the trophies and generally lend an air of decorum to the occasion. In the presence of Her Majesty, 'All competitors must be dressed in Highland costume, except for running and jumping', say the rules for the Braemar Gathering.

Although the gathering lasts all day, the Royal Family only arrive at 3.00p.m., stay for about an hour, then depart. Even so, their presence is what many people come to Braemar for: there are legions of elderly females, Queen Elizabeth-like in hats and coats, who bristle with indignation if the morning papers treat their heroes with anything less than deference. 'It's not right', they say, straining to see if Her Majesty is wearing the same kilted skirt she wore last time they saw her. Year after year, they come to Braemar in coaches, having run the gauntlet of motorway 'comfort stops' from places as far afield as Cheltenham and Harrogate. These are the stoics who stand outside shopping centres to catch 'just a glimpse' when Her Majesty arrives for the opening. This is her public, who faithfully book the ringside seats the year before the event in order that they might sit, sandwiches on rug on lap, not twenty feet from the presence incarcerated in its little wooden shed.

Some years, they hit the jackpot: the entire family is there. In others, they're not so lucky. In 1992 a much-depleted royal party consisted of the Queen, the Duke of Edinburgh, the Queen Mother and Prince Edward only. The hoped-for appearance of the Waleses and their children never happened and the Princess Royal avoided the limelight in the wake of her own troubled marriage. But a roaring 'God Save the Queen', echoing around the nearby hills, will have left Her Majesty in no doubt about where the loyalties of the day lay — more significantly than might otherwise be reckoned, given that a great many participants and spectators come from Australia, Canada, New Zealand and America.

There may possibly have been Highland gatherings on the Braes o' Mar for thousands of years — long before the first sporting events were held by King Malcolm. The evolution of the Braemar Gathering has been steady and continuous and of all the events of the Scottish Season, it is perhaps most steeped in tradition; here you see the ancient sporting pastimes of the Gael intact, if weathered. It may be a fairly slick event now that it has to cater for 20,000 spectators and has sponsors to keep it going, but there is no doubt that its long and venerable history is a continuing subject of fascination for all those who visit it.

INSIDER TIPS

★ Book tickets to the gathering in advance to avoid the long wait in the queue at the gates to the Memorial Park.

★ Book a hotel long in advance if you plan to weekend on Royal Deeside; Ballater and Banchory are the best towns to stay in.

★ Come prepared for all types of weather: it might pour; equally, temperatures might be tropical, as they were in 1991. Bring a kilt — if you have one. Here you see them in great profusion.

★ A hip flask filled with the local brew wouldn't be a bad idea.

★ Walking boots are essential.

INTERNATIONAL RUGBY, TWICKENHAM

OCTOBER — NOVEMBER

'ALL BLACKS ARE taking laws to absolute limits', shouted a large headline on the sporting pages of the London *Evening Standard* in November 1993. Eye-catching words such as these, delivered in bold black type, herald the start of another international rugby season of which the focus, in London at least, is Twickenham — rugby's own hallowed showground. This is also the start of winter and, in Twickenham's car park, the beginning of another alfresco dining experience and this time rain, mud and, preferably, temperatures just above zero, are its own particular hallmarks.

This is a bloody period in which lurid accounts of nose bleeds, concussion, stitches and broken limbs clutter up the back pages of the daily papers, along with reports of the antics of the New Zealand team, the All Blacks, rugby's love-to-hate *bête noire*. The paper's efforts to stir up some collective emotion over the steamroller tactics of the visiting team leave no stone unturned, its tone one that mixes indignation and incredulity with a kind of horrified fascination. After all, while Australia are the official world champions, when it comes to rugby gamesmanship New Zealand, with its huge players, are the undisputed leaders.

Gamesmanship? Every rugby team has a few tricks which it uses to gain an advantage on the field. It's just that the All Blacks have been accused of it more often than most for their blatant offside, for taking the support runner out of play and for late tackles. Their most infamous act ever came in 1978, when locks Andy Haden and Frank Oliver simultaneously 'dived' out of the line-out in the final minute against Cardiff. A penalty was awarded which was kicked successfully to give the All Blacks a controversial victory.

The New Zealand team label anyone who criticizes them a whinger and yet they have been very unhappy about claims of gamesmanship. 'At international level', continues the *Standard*, 'everyone is at it. The All Blacks are simply much better than anyone else.' They always have been and it makes a rugby match at Twickenham a thrilling experience — much like it must have been for the pagan hoi polloi of ancient Rome to watch an early Christian tackle a wild beast in the Colosseum. Only one could win and the ensuing

contest inevitably left one or both in a bloody mess: remember the Bridgend incident in 1978? Not only was J. P. R. Williams raked by the All Black forward John Ashworth, but one of the All Blacks was so severely injured it looked like his back ought to have been on a butcher's block. Like the spectacles in the Colosseum, this is part of Twickenham's fascination.

The *Evening Standard*'s report is accompanied by a colour photograph the subject of which is of a type that, out of sympathy for the victim depicted (in this case an English player hurtling backwards under the full force of a late challenge from his opponent, an All Black), causes a sharp intake of breath in the reader. Said victim might just as well have been delivered an unsportsmanlike, nasty knee-jerk in the groin. Whichever, the reader's action will have been the same: an agonized roll-about on the floor — or the tiers of Twickenham's grandstand — and a howl in painful empathy. The sacrificial victim's arms are flying about and his legs are inelegantly splayed outwards as he is tipped upside down by the force. If the picture could speak, the air around him would be blue and it generally is in the muddy slush of the playing field.

'If you put yourself on the opposition side of a ruck,' says Chris Jones, a sports correspondent for the *Standard*, 'then it is accepted in New Zealand you will receive a "tickle of the sprigs". In Britain we would describe it as a good shoeing but the effects on the body are the same.' Phil de Glanville would agree: he needed fifteen stitches around the left eye after he was savaged by the opposition from down under in the match against Midlands at Leicester in 1993.

Menace and aggression are the hallmarks of this game, though contrary to what you might expect, all of this is somehow sublimated by the spectators who, generally, are an angelic bunch not given to the type of hooliganism and yobbish behaviour attendant on the average football match at home and abroad. It has been reported that crowd violence has yet to rear its ugly head at Twickenham.

Might this have something to do with the fact that rugby is, essentially, an amateur game? The stakes have to do with prestige and honour and rollicking good play — in addition to the fact that nearly all of those present have probably played the game at

some time in their lives and are living out the scrums and the high kicks happening down there on the field, or imagining themselves covered in glory following a particularly magnificent try. They are watching technique and wishing that they, too, were out there on the muddy field of play. Bashing a supporter of the opposing team on the head with a broken bottle isn't really rugby.

Over 30,000 pints of beer, provided by caterers from a variety of tents and old buses, are consumed at Twickenham during the course of a single afternoon. Forget that wine, champagne, whisky and ale — as well as beer — are also downed during the picnic in the car park, the scene of virtually every Season's event's 'other' life. It's all consumed in honour of the Great Day Out. Arrival before start of play is marked by the clatter of portable barbecue sets and calor gas stoves, as preparations for lunch are underway round at the back of the Bentley or on the open bootflap of the Range Rover. Things are quieter in the vicinity of the Toyotas and the Cortinas, in which occupants are 'indoors', arranged around a six-pack, a flask of tea and a sackful of bacon butties. From the steamed-up car, their view of the neighbours, with their rugs and blankets and bits of plastic, and chops, sausages and steaks barbecuing and steak-and-kidney pies warming up, is obscured. Chrome flasks with leather handles are filled with hot soup or sausages, and there are coffee and whisky pick-me-ups.

Like any other event of the Season, this other life is the single most important side-attraction beyond the day's sporting focus. It is never as gripping as the entertainment on the field. After all, who could go wrong with a philosophy like that of the All Blacks: to entertain and, hopefully, to win.

INSIDER TIPS

♦ Take warm, waterproof clothes.

♦ A hip flask is essential. Don't go without it.

♦ Life will be a lot easier if you take public transport to Twickenham, which is only ten miles from the centre of London.

♦ If you must go by car, start early, otherwise monumental traffic jams will frustrate your attempts to arrive on time. Get there by 11.00a.m.

♦ Think about buying tickets for the international season as early as April.

Essential Addresses and Ticket Information

The information below was correct at the time of publication. However, details such as ticket prices and opening times often change. For up-to-the-minute information, contact The British Tourist Authority, 12 Regent Street, London SW1Y 4PQ Telephone: 071-730 3400.

The Chelsea Flower Show
Royal Hospital
Royal Hospital Road
Chelsea
London SW3

Tickets:
The Royal Horticultural Society
80 Vincent Square
London SW1P 2PE
Telephone: 071-834 4333
(information only)
Enclose a stamped addressed envelope. Tickets are strictly limited and there are no sales at the gate.

The Royal Academy
Summer Exhibition
The Royal Academy of Art
Burlington House
Piccadilly
London W1V ODS
Telephone: 071-439 7438
(information)
Telephone: 071-439 4996/7
(recorded message about current exhibitions)

Open: 10am to 6pm
Admission charge to most exhibitions

The Derby Stakes, Epsom
Information, tickets and car park reservations:
The Grandstand
Epsom Downs
Surrey KT18 5LQ
Telephone: 03727 26311

Trooping the Colour
Tickets:
The Brigade Major
Household Division
HQ London District
Chelsea Barracks
London SW1H 8RF
Telephone: 071-414 2357
Tickets — you are allowed two per person — are allocated by ballot. Apply in writing between 1 January and 28 February, enclosing a stamped addressed envelope or international reply coupon. If you are not selected, you may be offered tickets for the rehearsal.

Royal Ascot
Tickets, Royal Enclosure:
Her Majesty's Representative
Ascot Office
St James's Place
London SW1A 1BP
Telephone: 071-930 9882
The list opens in January and you

must apply in writing. In theory, anyone can get in, but you must be sponsored by one other who has already been in the Royal Enclosure at least eight times. You can apply for as many tickets as you like, as long as they are for immediate members of the family.

Tickets, General:
Ascot Authority
Ascot Racecourse
Ascot
Berkshire SL5 7JN
Telephone: 0344 22211
Tickets available from 1 January

The All England Lawn Tennis Championships, Wimbledon
Tickets:
The All England Lawn Tennis & Croquet Club
P.O. Box 98
Church Road
Wimbledon
London SW19 5AE
Tickets, particularly for Centre and No. 1 Courts, are much in demand and are allocated by ballot. Apply for an application form (one per address only) between 1 September and 31 December, enclosing a stamped addressed envelope.

THE HENLEY ROYAL REGATTA
Tickets:
Henley Royal Regatta
Regatta Headquarters
Henley-on-Thames
Oxfordshire RG9 2LY
Telephone: 0491 572153
Members only are allowed in the
Stewards' Enclosure; anyone can
apply for tickets to the
Regatta Enclosure.

INTERNATIONAL CRICKET, LORD'S
Tickets:
Lord's Cricket Ground
St John's Wood
London NW8 8QN
Telephone: 071-289 1611
(general enquiries)
Telephone: 071-289 5005
(credit card bookings)

THE ROYAL WELSH SHOW —
SIOE FRENHINOL CYMRU —
BUILTH WELLS
Tickets:
The Royal Welsh
Agricultural Society Ltd
Llanelwedd
Builth Wells
Powys LD2 3SY
Telephone: 0982 553683
Show is open 8am to 9pm.
daily

INTERNATIONAL POLO, WINDSOR
Tickets:
Guards Polo Club

in Windsor Great Park
Englefield Road
Egham
Surrey TW20 0HP
Telephone: 0784 437797

*Information about fixtures also
available from:*
The Hurlingham Polo Association
Winterlake
Kirtlington
Kidlington
Oxon OX5 3HG
Telephone: 08693 50044
Tickets for the Cartier tent and
Guards Club Enclosure are
available through Keith Prowse.
Telephone: 081-795 2222

GLORIOUS GOODWOOD
Goodwood House
Goodwood
Chichester
West Sussex PO18 0PY
Telephone: 0243 774107
The House is open April to
September, Sunday and Monday
only, plus Tuesdays and
Thursdays in August. Telephone
before visiting, as opening hours
may vary.
Racecourse: address and
telephone number as above
for information.

COWES WEEK
*Tourist information,
accommodation, tickets for Ocean*

*World Crew Ball (£15 a head),
Cowes Week Ball (£55 a head):*
Telephone: 0983 291914 (closed
Monday and Thursday)

Cowes Yacht Haven
Telephone: 0983 299975
Small admission charge

TEA AT BETTY'S CAFE TEA ROOMS,
HARROGATE
1 Parliament Street
Harrogate
North Yorkshire HG1 2QU
Telephone: 0423 502746
Open 9am to 9pm.

Betty's is also at:
York
6—8 St Helen's Square
Telephone: 0904 659142
Open 9am to 9pm.

Ilkley
32—34 The Grove
Telephone: 0943 608029
Open 9am to 6pm.

Northallerton
188 High Street
Telephone: 0609 775154
Open 9am to 5.30pm.

Betty's by post:
Catalogue and order forms can be
obtained from the Harrogate Tea
Rooms, address as above.
Telephone orders: 0423 531211.

BUCKINGHAM PALACE
Tickets:
It is only possible to buy tickets (no more than four adult tickets per person) on the day from the ticket office in Pall Mall. Only a certain number of tickets are available each day and are sold in sequence. It is therefore not possible to buy tickets for the visiting time of your choice. Visitors in the queue are informed of the approximate queuing time and, in particular, if they will not be able to buy a ticket for entry to the palace that day. Therein lies the flaw: you might spend time queuing and get no tickets at all.
Telephone: 071-930 5526 (Buckingham Palace enquiries office) for general information.

THE EDINBURGH
INTERNATIONAL FESTIVAL
Festival Box Office
21 Market Street
Edinburgh EH1 1BW
Telephone: 031-225 5756
(tickets and information)
Ticket office opens in April

The Fringe
180 High Street
Edinburgh EH1 1QS
Telephone: 031-226 5257/9
(all year round information)

Telephone: 031-226 5138
(credit card bookings)

A Fringe programme is available for the price of postage only.

The Tattoo
22 Market Street
Edinburgh EH1 1QB
Telephone: 031-225 1188
(tickets and information)
Telephone: 031-225 3661
(credit card bookings)

The Film Festival
The Filmhouse
88 Lothian Road
Edinburgh EH3 9BZ
Telephone: 031-228 4051
(tickets and information)
Telephone: 031-229 2550
(credit card bookings)

The Jazz Festival
Tickets and programmes available from the Fringe Office.
Telephone: 031-650 8200
(tickets and information)

The Book Festival
Scottish Book Centre
137 Dundee Street
Edinburgh EH11 1BG
Telephone: 031-228 5444
(information)
The Book Festival is held every two years, the next one in 1995.

CHATSWORTH, DERBYSHIRE
Chatsworth
Bakewell
Derbyshire DE45 1PP
Telephone: 0246 582204
(information)
Open: late March to end October
House: 11am to 4.30pm.
Gardens: 11am to 5pm.
Admission charge

THE ARUNDEL ARTS FESTIVAL
The Arundel Festival Society
The Mary Gate
Arundel
Sussex BN18 9AT
Telephone: 0903 883690
(information)
Send a stamped addressed envelope for information and booking forms.

Box Office
Telephone: 0903 883474
(open a month before and during festival only)

Arundel Castle
Open: Sunday to Friday,
11am to 5pm.
Admission charge

ALTON TOWERS
Alton
Staffordshire ST10 4DB
Telephone: 0538 702200
(general enquiries)
Open: late March to end October
Grounds and gardens open at
9am, rides and attractions at
10am.

THE ILLUMINATIONS, BLACKPOOL
Blackpool Tourist
Information Centre
1 Clifton Street
Blackpool SY1 1LY
Telephone: 0253 21623
(information)

THE ROYAL HIGHLAND GAMES,
BRAEMAR
Tickets:
The Bookings Secretary
B.R.H.S.
Coilacriech
Ballater
Aberdeenshire AB35 5UH
Telephone: 03397 55377
(information)
Enclose a stamped addressed
envelope. Overseas visitors
should include the equivalent of
£5 to cover bank charges plus
return air postage of tickets.

INTERNATIONAL RUGBY,
TWICKENHAM
Tickets:
It is easiest to get tickets if you
already belong to a rugby club
and apply for tickets through it.
However, on the morning of the
game, tickets and returns are on
sale at Twickenham; but numbers
are limited, so get there early.
Otherwise, check with the Rugby
Football Union.
Telephone: 081-891 2333.

ACKNOWLEDGEMENTS

We are most grateful to all those
who read the text and suggested
changes and amendments —
above all Anne Engel, Madeleine
Masson and Liz Walker. We
would also like to thank Allan
Manham (The Artworks);
designer Andrew Barron;
Christine Newson, and Vivien
Bowler (of Little, Brown and
Company), all of whom gave
much advice and help way
beyond the call of duty; and, of
course, Royal Mail.
   We are indebted to the
British Tourist Authority for
generously giving us not only
advice, but also copious
quantities of maps and brochures.
In addition, a great many others
provided tickets, programmes
and background information
which helped smooth our path
through the shires in search of
the true British Season: Marcus
von Ackermann; Shari-Jane Boda
(Alton Towers); Sue Bond (Sue
Bond Public Relations); Pilar
Boxford (Cartier); Braemar Royal
Highland Society; Buckingham
Palace Press Office; Vanessa De
Lisle; the organizers of the Derby
Stakes; Tessa Katz; Gordon
McCulloch (Edinburgh
Marketing); the Marylebone
Cricket Club; Helen Nicholson;
the organizers of the Royal Welsh
Show; Mary Tebje (Madame
Tussaud's); The All England
Lawn Tennis & Croquet Club.